HOW
TO BE A
CHRISTIAN

ALSO BY C. S. LEWIS

A Grief Observed

George MacDonald: An Anthology

Mere Christianity

Miracles

The Abolition of Man

The Great Divorce

The Problem of Pain

The Screwtape Letters

The Weight of Glory

The Four Loves

Till We Have Faces

Surprised by Joy: The Shape of My Early Life

Reflections on the Psalms

Letters to Malcolm: Chiefly on Prayer

Personal Heresy

The World's Last Night and Other Essays

Poems

The Dark Tower and Other Stories

HOW
TO BE A
CHRISTIAN

REFLECTIONS AND ESSAYS

C. S. Lewis

HarperOne
An Imprint of HarperCollinsPublishers

HarperOne

HarperCollins books may be purchased for educational, business, or
sales promotional use. For information, please email the Special Markets
Department at SPsales@harpercollins.com.

FIRST EDITION

Designed by Yvonne Chan

Library of Congress Cataloging-in-Publication Data is available upon
request.

ISBN 978-0-06-284993-9

18 19 20 21 22   LSC   10 9 8 7 6 5 4 3 2 1

CONTENTS

Contents

Contents

ON WHAT IT MEANS TO BE PART
OF THE BODY OF CHRIST

ON PRACTICAL MATTERS ON BEING
A CHRISTIAN TODAY

SOURCE WORKS

PREFACE

CHRISTIANS SPEND A lot of time talking about beliefs and doctrines; so much so that one might think that mastering the faith is understanding a set of ideas. But that is not the case. The real substance of the faith dwells in the world of action. Christian faith becomes real when it is lived out. For example, being a Christian entails learning how to be slow to judge others and to check first the log in our own eye; how to quit focusing merely on our fears and worries in order to see how we can treat others as we would wish to be treated; how to reign in our anxieties about tomorrow and dampen our anger before it becomes a sin; how, when we are aggrieved, we forgive others.

Yes, doctrines are extremely important. Christians need to grapple with beliefs before we understand that we are empowered by Jesus to live in a new way. But understanding these ideas is a doorway, one that requires us to start walking in order for the ideas to have any meaning. Even the apostle Paul, the grandfather of most Christian theology, reminds us that faith, even if perfect, ends up a mere clanging bell if it is without love. And love can only be expressed by actions.

I say all this because (1) this is what I learned from C. S. Lewis and (2), ironically, Lewis is best known as the foremost defender of Christian ideas in the twentieth century. In other words, one might assume that Lewis might be a main cause for the notion that Christianity is essentially a body of ideas, given the success of his apologetical works, but that would be missing the nature of his ideas.

When I meet with scholars and theologians, almost all of them confess that Lewis played a significant role on their path toward their vocation. Yet, despite his popularity, when it comes to whose work scholars study, we hear the names of Barth, Hauerwas, Bonhoeffer, Wright, Pagels, Armstrong, Ehrman, and others, but seldom Lewis. I attend the annual joint conventions of the American Academy of Religion and the Society of Biblical Literature, where twenty thousand religion scholars descend on that year's metropolis and hold sessions on every arcane subject you could imagine (and many I could not imagine), and yet I am surprised how seldom the name "C. S. Lewis" shows up on the schedule. Why is that?

I think it is because Lewis never presented his ideas as some new heroic paradigm but only as a summary of "mere" Christianity, what most Christians have always believed. And Lewis's wisdom does not work best as a "grand theory" but rather as, what I would call, "wisdom on the journey." In other words, it is only by walking down the path of the Christian life that what he teaches seems to make sense and become "useful."

I still remember the light bulb going off when reading Book 4 in *Mere Christianity* where Lewis explains that by becoming a Christian we have signed on to the task of God making us perfect and anything short of this sometimes-painful process would be admitting that God is willing to give up on us, that God does not love us fully. Well, that ordered my young mind in a whole new way, reminding me that "becoming a Christian" was a path, not a one-time event, and that those closest to me and thus most affected by my imperfections, would be the main classroom God uses in this clean-up operation.

Another light-bulb moment was reading Screwtape's masterful meditation on gluttony. I had always thought of gluttony as a ravenous obese soul devouring everything in his path—i.e., not me. But in *The Screwtape Letters,* Lewis uses the human subject's mother and her lustful obsession with wanting "a slice of bread properly toasted" as the model of gluttony. Maybe I wasn't as "non-gluttonous" as I had thought. It is in these moments, when dealing with the nittygritty of what it means to live out the Christian faith, that Lewis's insights seem so deep, rich, and helpful.

The best example of what I am getting at comes in chapter 12 in *The Great Divorce* where the main character witnesses the spectacle of a heavenly parade with shining angels, saints, and animals flowing and dancing around a luminous woman who was so beautiful she was almost "unbearable" to behold. At first the observer thinks she must be Eve or Mary, the mother of Jesus. But he is told that, no, it is Sarah Smith, who lived as a suburban London housewife. In heaven, though, she is counted as one of the "great ones." How did she get this status? Because in her ordinary life, she became mother to every young man, woman, boy, girl, dog, or cat she encountered, loving them all in a way that made them more loveable and more eager to love others.

Not only did this chapter reset my calculations of what it means to be "great" as a Christian, it also helps us to understand Lewis's writings as whole. Lewis sought to help, encourage, and enlighten his readers about the Christian faith, especially in the ways it is seen by others as outdated or out of synch with our modern times. And in those endeavors he was masterful and more successful than he ever imagined. And part of the reason for his success was the fact that instead of desiring to be a great apologist and theologian, he measured himself by how closely he resembled Sarah Smith. And it was because of this humble approach that he did indeed, unknowingly, become a great apologist and theologian.

In this collection, we have gathered selections from chapters, essays, letters, and speeches from a wide range of Lewis's books, all having to do with how we live out our beliefs and not just how we believe. *How to Be a Christian* would not have been possible without the work of Zachry Kincaid, who gathered many of these pieces for us. Our hope is that in this book you will not only encounter new pieces by Lewis, but that you will also discover new wisdom for the journey, the kind that will help us become a little more like Sarah Smith.

MICHAEL G. MAUDLIN
Senior vice president and executive editor
HarperOne

ON WORKING OUT
YOUR SALVATION

WHAT GOD CARES about is not exactly our actions. What he cares about is that we should be creatures of a certain kind or quality—the kind of creatures He intended us to be—creatures related to Himself in a certain way. I do not add 'and related to one another in a certain way', because that is included: if you are right with Him you will inevitably be right with all your fellow creatures, just as if all the spokes of a wheel are fitted rightly into the hub and the rim they are bound to be in the right positions to one another. And as long as a man is thinking of God as an

---

Mere Christianity, from the chapter titled "Faith."

examiner who has set him a sort of paper to do, or as the opposite party in a sort of bargain—as long as he is thinking of claims and counter-claims between himself and God—he is not yet in the right relation to Him. He is misunderstanding what he is and what God is. And he cannot get into the right relation until he has discovered the fact of our bankruptcy.

When I say 'discovered', I mean really discovered: not simply said it parrot-fashion. Of course, any child, if given a certain kind of religious education, will soon learn to say that we have nothing to offer to God that is not already His own and that we find ourselves failing to offer even that without keeping something back. But I am talking of really discovering this: really finding out by experience that it is true.

Now we cannot, in that sense, discover our failure to keep God's law except by trying our very hardest (and then failing). Unless we really try, whatever we say there will always be at the back of our minds the idea that if we try harder next time we shall succeed in being completely good. Thus, in one sense, the road back to God is a road of moral effort, of trying harder and harder. But in another sense it is not trying that is ever going to bring us home. All this trying leads up to the vital moment at which you turn to God and say, 'You must do this. I can't.' Do not, I implore you, start asking yourselves, 'Have I reached that moment?' Do not sit down and start watching your own mind to see if it is coming along. That puts a man quite on the wrong track. When the most important things in our life happen we quite often do not know, at the moment, what is going on. A man does not always say to himself, 'Hullo! I'm growing up.' It is often only when he looks back that he realises what has happened and recognises it as what people call 'growing up'. You can see it even in simple matters. A man who starts anxiously watching to see whether he is going to sleep is very likely to remain wide awake. As well, the thing I am talking of now may not happen to every one in a sudden flash—as it did to St. Paul or Bunyan: it may be so gradual that no one could ever point to a particular hour or even a particular year. And what matters is the nature of the change in itself, not how we feel while it is happening. It is the change from being confident about our own efforts to the state in which we despair of doing anything for ourselves and leave it to God.

I know the words 'leave it to God' can be misunderstood, but they must stay for the moment. The sense in which a Christian leaves it to God is that he puts all his trust in Christ: trusts that Christ will somehow share with him the perfect human obedience which He carried out from His birth to His crucifixion: that Christ will make the man more like Himself and, in a sense, make good his deficiencies. In Christian language, He will share His 'sonship' with us, will make us, like Himself, 'Sons of God': in Book IV I shall attempt to analyse the meaning of those words a little further. If you like to put it that way, Christ offers something for nothing: He even offers everything for nothing. In a sense, the whole Christian life consists in accepting that very remarkable offer. But the difficulty is to reach the point of recognising that all we have done and can do is nothing. What we should have liked would be for God to count our good points and ignore our bad ones. Again, in a sense, you may say that no temptation is ever overcome until we stop trying to overcome it—throw up the sponge. But then you could not 'stop trying' in the right way and for the right reason until you had tried your very hardest. And, in yet another sense, handing everything over to Christ does not, of course, mean that you stop trying. To trust Him means, of course, trying to do all that He says. There would be no sense in saying you trusted a person if you would not take his advice. Thus if you have really handed yourself over to Him, it must follow that you are trying to obey Him. But trying in a new way, a less worried way. Not doing these things in order to be saved, but because He has begun to save you already. Not hoping to get to Heaven as a reward for your actions, but inevitably wanting to act in a certain way because a first faint gleam of Heaven is already inside you.

Christians have often disputed as to whether what leads the Christian home is good actions, or Faith in Christ. I have no right really to speak on such a difficult question, but it does seem to me like asking which blade in a pair of scissors is most necessary. A serious moral effort is the only thing that will bring you to the point where you throw up the sponge. Faith in Christ is the only thing to save you from despair at that point: and out of that Faith in Him good actions must inevitably come. There are two parodies of the truth which different sets of Christians have, in the past, been accused by other Christians of believing: perhaps they may make the truth clearer. One set were accused of saying, 'Good actions are all that matters. The best good action is charity. The best kind of charity is giving money. The best thing to give money to is the Church. So hand us over £10,000 and we will see you through.' The answer to that nonsense, of course, would be that good actions done for that motive, done with the idea that Heaven can be bought, would not be good actions at all, but only commercial speculations. The other set were accused of saying, 'Faith is all that matters. Consequently, if you have faith, it doesn't matter what you do. Sin away, my lad, and have a good time and Christ will see that it makes no difference in the end.' The answer to that nonsense is that, if what you call your 'faith' in Christ does not involve taking the slightest notice of what He says, then it is not Faith at all—not faith or trust in Him, but only intellectual acceptance of some theory about Him.

The Bible really seems to clinch the matter when it puts the two things together into one amazing sentence. The first half is, 'Work out your own salvation with fear and trembling'—which looks as if everything depended on us and our good actions: but the second half goes on, 'For it is God who worketh in you'—which looks as if God did everything and we nothing. I am afraid that is the sort of thing we come up against in Christianity. I am puzzled, but I am not surprised. You see, we are now trying to understand, and to separate into water-tight compartments, what exactly God does and what man does when God and man are working together. And, of course, we begin by thinking it is like two men working together, so that you could say, 'He did this bit and I did that.' But this way of thinking breaks down. God is not like that. He is inside you as well as outside: even if we could understand who did what, I do not think human language could properly express it. In the attempt to express it different Churches say different things. But you will find that even those who insist most strongly on the importance of good actions tell you you need Faith; and even those who insist most strongly on Faith tell you to do good actions. At any rate that is as far as I can go.

I think all Christians would agree with me if I said that though Christianity seems at the first to be all about morality, all about duties and rules and guilt and virtue, yet it leads you on, out of all that, into something beyond. One has a glimpse of a country where they do not talk of those things, except perhaps as a joke. Every one there is filled full with what we should call goodness as a mirror is filled with light. But they do not call it goodness. They do not call it anything. They are not thinking of it. They are too busy looking at the source from which it comes. But this is near the stage where the road passes over the rim of our world. No one's eyes can see very far beyond that: lots of people's eyes can see further than mine.

ON BEING CONCERNED
ABOUT MORE THAN THE
SALVATION OF SOULS

WE HAVE ALWAYS to answer the question: 'How can you be so frivolous and selfish as to think about anything but the salvation of human souls?' and we have, at the moment, to answer the additional question, 'How can you be so frivolous and selfish as to think of anything but the war?' Now part of our answer will be the same for both questions. The one implies that our life can, and ought, to become exclusively and explicitly religious: the other, that it can

---

The Weight of Glory, from the chapter titled "Learning in War-Time."

and ought to become exclusively national. I believe that our whole life can, and indeed must, become religious in a sense to be explained later. But if it is meant that all our activities are to be of the kind that can be recognized as 'sacred' and opposed to secular', then I would give a single reply to both my imaginary assailants. I would say, 'Whether it ought to happen or not, the thing you are recommending is not going to happen.' Before I became a Christian I do not think I fully realised that one's life, after conversion, would inevitably consist in doing most of the same things one had been doing before, one hopes, in a new spirit, but still the same things. Before I went to the last war I certainly expected that my life in the trenches would, in some mysterious sense, be all war. In fact, I found that the nearer you got to the front line the less everyone spoke and thought of the allied cause and the progress of the campaign; and I am pleased to find that Tolstoi, in the greatest war book ever written, records the same thing and so, in its own way, does the *Iliad*. Neither conversion nor enlistment in the army is really going to obliterate our human life. Christians and soldiers are still men: the infidel's idea of a religious life, and the civilian's idea of active service, are fantastic. If you attempted, in either case, to suspend your whole intellectual and aesthetic activity, you would only succeed in substituting a worse cultural life for a better. You are not, in fact, going to read nothing, either in the Church or in the line: if you don't read good books you will read bad ones. If you don't go on thinking rationally, you will think irrationally. If you reject aesthetic satisfactions you will fall into sensual satisfactions.

There is therefore this analogy between the claims of our religion and the claims of the war: neither of them, for most of us, will simply cancel or remove from the slate the merely human life which we were leading before we entered them. But they will operate in this way for different reasons. The war will fail to absorb our whole attention because it is a finite object, and therefore, intrinsically unfitted to support the whole attention of a human soul. In order to avoid misunderstanding I must here make a few distinctions. I believe our cause to be, as human causes go, very righteous, and I therefore believe it to be a duty to participate in this war. And every duty is a religious duty, and our obligation to perform every duty is therefore absolute. Thus we may have a duty to rescue a drowning man, and perhaps, if we live on a dangerous coast, to learn lifesaving so as to be ready for any drowning man when he turns up. It may be our duty to lose our own lives in saving him. But if anyone devoted himself to lifesaving in the sense of giving it his total attention—so that he thought and spoke of nothing else and demanded the cessation of all other human activities until everyone had learned to swim—he would be a monomaniac. The rescue of drowning men is, then, a duty worth dying for, but not worth living for. It seems to me that all political duties (among which I include military duties) are of this kind. A man may have to die for our country: but no man must, in any exclusive sense, live for his country. He who surrenders himself without reservation to the temporal claims of a nation, or a party, or a class is rendering to Caesar that which, of all things, most emphatically belongs to God: himself.

It is for a very different reason that religion cannot occupy the whole of life in the sense of excluding all our natural activities. For, of course, in some sense, it must occupy the whole of life. There is no question of a compromise between the claims of God and the claims of culture, or politics, or anything else. God's claim is infinite and inexorable. You can refuse it: or you can begin to try to grant it. There is no middle way. Yet in spite of this it is clear that Christianity does not exclude any of the ordinary human activities. St. Paul tells people to get on with their jobs. He even assumes that Christians may go to dinner parties, and, what is more, dinner parties given by pagans. Our Lord attends a wedding and provides miraculous wine. Under the aegis of His Church, and in the most Christian ages, learning and the arts flourish. The solution of this paradox is, of course, well known to you. 'Whether ye eat or drink or whatsoever ye do, do all to the glory of God.'

All our merely natural activities will be accepted, if they are offered to God, even the humblest, and all of them, even the noblest, will be sinful if they are not. Christianity does not simply replace our natural life and substitute a new one; it is rather a new organisation which exploits, to its own supernatural ends, these natural materials. No doubt, in a given situation, it demands the surrender of some, or of all, our merely human pursuits; it is better to be saved with one eye, than, having two, to be cast into Gehenna. But it does this, in a sense, *per accidens*—because, in those special circumstances, it has ceased to be possible to practise this or that activity to the glory of God. There is no essential quarrel between the spiritual life and the human activities as such. Thus the omnipresence of obedience to God in a Christian's life is, in a way, analogous to the omnipresence of God in space. God does not fill space as a body fills it, in the sense that parts of Him are in different parts of space, excluding other objects from them. Yet He is everywhere—totally present at every point of space—according to good theologians.

We are now in a position to answer the view that human culture is an inexcusable frivolity on the part of creatures loaded with such awful responsibilities as we. I reject at once an idea which lingers in the mind of some modern people that cultural activities are in their own right spiritual and meritorious—as though scholars and poets were intrinsically more pleasing to God than scavengers and bootblacks. I think it was Matthew Arnold who first used the English word *spiritual* in the sense of the German *geistlich*, and so inaugurated this most dangerous and most anti-Christian error. Let us clear it forever from our minds. The work of a Beethoven, and the work of a charwoman, become spiritual on precisely the same condition, that of being offered to God, of being done humbly 'as to the Lord'. This does not, of course, mean that it is for anyone a mere toss-up whether he should sweep rooms or compose symphonies. A mole must dig to the glory of God and a cock must crow. We are members of one body, but differentiated members, each with his own vocation. A man's upbringing, his talents, his circumstances, are usually a tolerable index of his vocation. If our parents have sent us to Oxford, if our country allows us to remain there, this is *prima facie* evidence that the life which we, at any rate, can best lead to the glory of God at present is the learned life. By leading that life to the glory of God I do not, of course, mean any attempt to make our intellectual inquiries work out to edifying conclusions. That would be, as Bacon says, to offer to the author of truth the unclean sacrifice of a lie. I mean the pursuit of knowledge and beauty, in a sense, for their own sake, but in a sense which does not exclude their being for God's sake. An appetite for these things exists in the human mind, and God makes no appetite in vain. We can therefore pursue knowledge as such, and beauty as such, in the sure confidence that by so doing we are either advancing to the vision of God ourselves or indirectly helping others to do so. Humility, no less than the appetite, encourages us to concentrate simply on the knowledge or the beauty, not too much concerning ourselves with their ultimate relevance to the vision of God. That relevance may not be intended for us but for our betters—for men who come after and find the spiritual significance of what we dug out in blind and humble obedience to our vocation. This is the teleological argument that the existence of the impulse and the faculty prove that they must have a proper function in God's scheme—the argument by which Thomas Aquinas proves that sexuality would have existed even without the Fall. The soundness of the argument, as regards culture, is proved by experience. The intellectual life is not the only road to God, nor the safest, but we find it to be a road, and it may be the appointed road for us. Of course, it will be so only so long as we keep the impulse pure and disinterested. That is the great difficulty. As the author of the *Theologia Germanica* says, we may come to love knowledge—our knowing—more than the thing known: to delight not in the exercise of our talents but in the fact that they are ours, or even in the reputation they bring us. Every success in the scholar's life increases this danger. If it becomes irresistible, he must give up his scholarly work. The time for plucking out the right eye has arrived.

ON THE DANGERS OF
POINTING OUT
FAULTS IN OTHERS

I SUPPOSE I may assume that seven out of ten of those who read these lines are in some kind of difficulty about some other human being. Either at work or at home, either the people who employ you or those whom you employ, either those who share your house or those whose house you share, either your in-laws or parents or children, your wife or your husband, are making life harder for you than it need be even in these days. It is to be hoped that we do not often mention

---

God in the Dock, from the chapter titled
"The Trouble with 'X'. . . ."

these difficulties (especially the domestic ones) to outsiders. But sometimes we do. An outside friend asks us
why we are looking so glum, and the truth comes out.

On such occasions the outside friend usually says,
'But why don't you tell them? Why don't you go to
your wife (or husband, or father, or daughter, or boss,
or landlady, or lodger) and have it all out? People are
usually reasonable. All you've got to do is to make
them see things in the right light. Explain it to them
in a reasonable, quiet, friendly way.' And we, whatever we say outwardly, think sadly to ourselves, 'He
doesn't know "X."' We do. We know how utterly
hopeless it is to make 'X' see reason. Either we've
tried it over and over again—tried it till we are sick
of trying it—or else we've never tried it because we
saw from the beginning how useless it would be. We
know that if we attempt to 'have it all out with "X"'
there will either be a 'scene,' or else 'X' will stare at
us in blank amazement and say, 'I don't know what on
earth you're talking about'; or else (which is perhaps
worst of all) 'X' will quite agree with us and promise

to turn over a new leaf and put everything on a new footing—and then, twenty-four hours later, will be exactly the same as 'X' has always been.

You know, in fact, that any attempt to talk things over with 'X' will shipwreck on the old, fatal flaw in 'X's' character. And you see, looking back, how all the plans you have ever made always have shipwrecked on that fatal flaw—on 'X's' incurable jealousy, or laziness, or touchiness, or muddleheadedness, or bossiness, or ill temper, or changeableness. Up to a certain age you have perhaps had the illusion that some external stroke of good fortune—an improvement in health, a rise of salary, the end of the war—would solve your difficulty. But you know better now. The war is over, and you realise that even if the other things happened, 'X' would still be 'X', and you would still be up against the same old problem. Even if you became a millionaire, your husband would still be a bully, or your wife would still nag or your son would still drink, or you'd still have to have your mother-in-law to live with you.

It is a great step forward to realise that this is so; to face the fact that even if all external things went right, real happiness would still depend on the character of the people you have to live with—and that you can't alter their characters. And now comes the point. When you have seen this you have, for the first time, had a glimpse of what it must be like for God. For, of course, this is (in one way) just what God Himself is up against. He has provided a rich, beautiful world for people to live in. He has given them intelligence to show them how it can be used, and conscience to show them how it ought to be used. He has contrived that the things they need for their biological life (food, drink, rest, sleep, exercise) should be positively delightful to them. And, having done all this, He then sees all His plans spoiled—just as our little plans are spoiled—by the crookedness of the people themselves. All the things He has given them to be happy with they turn into occasions for quarreling and jealousy, and excess and hoarding, and tomfoolery.

You may say it is very different for God because He could, if He pleased, alter people's characters, and we can't. But this difference doesn't go quite as deep as we may at first think. God has made it a rule for Himself that He won't alter people's character by force. He can and will alter them—but only if the people will let Him. In that way He has really and truly limited His power. Sometimes we wonder why He has done so, or even wish that He hadn't. But apparently He thinks it worth doing. He would rather have a world of free beings, with all its risks, than a world of people who did right like machines because they couldn't do anything else. The more we succeed in imagining what a world of perfect automatic beings would be like, the more, I think, we shall see His wisdom.

I said that when we see how all our plans shipwreck on the characters of the people we have to deal with, we are 'in *one* way' seeing what it must be like for God. But only in one way. There are two respects in which God's view must be very different from ours. In the first place, He sees (like you) how all the people in your home or your job are in various degrees awkward or difficult; but when He looks into that home or factory or office He sees one more person of the same kind—the one you never do see. I mean, of course, yourself. That is the next great step in wisdom—to realise that you also are just that sort of person. You also have a fatal flaw in your character. All the hopes and plans of others have again and again shipwrecked on your character just as your hopes and plans have shipwrecked on theirs.

It is no good passing this over with some vague, general admission such as 'Of course, I know I have my faults.' It is important to realise that there is some really fatal flaw in you: something which gives the others just that same feeling of *despair* which their flaws give you. And it is almost certainly something you don't know about—like what the advertisements call 'halitosis', which everyone notices except the person who has it. But why, you ask, don't the others tell me? Believe me, they have tried to tell you over and over again, and you just couldn't 'take it.' Perhaps a good deal of what you call their 'nagging' or 'bad temper' or 'queerness' are just their attempts to make you see the truth. And even the faults you do know you don't know fully. You say, 'I admit I lost my temper last night'; but the others know that you're always doing it, that you are a bad-tempered person. You say, 'I admit I drank too much last Saturday'; but every one else knows that you are an habitual drunkard.

That is one way in which God's view must differ from mine. He sees all the characters: I see all except my own. But the second difference is this. He loves the people in spite of their faults. He goes on loving. He does not let go. Don't say, 'It's all very well for Him; He hasn't got to live with them.' He has. He is inside them as well as outside them. He is *with* them far more intimately and closely and incessantly than we can ever be. Every vile thought within their minds (and ours), every moment of spite, envy, arrogance, greed, and self-conceit comes right up against His patient and longing love, and grieves His spirit more than it grieves ours.

The more we can imitate God in both these respects, the more progress we shall make. We must love 'X' more; and we must learn to see ourselves as a person of exactly the same kind. Some people say it is morbid to be always thinking of one's own faults. That would be all very well if most of us could stop thinking of our own without soon beginning to think about those of other people. For unfortunately we *enjoy* thinking about other people's faults: and in the proper sense of the word 'morbid', that is the most morbid pleasure in the world.

We don't like rationing which is imposed upon us, but I suggest one form of rationing which we ought to impose on ourselves. Abstain from all thinking about other people's faults, unless your duties as a teacher or parent make it necessary to think about them. Whenever the thoughts come unnecessarily into one's mind, why not simply shove them away? And think of one's own faults instead? For there, with God's help, one *can* do something. Of all the awkward people in your house or job there is only one whom you can improve very much. That is the practical end at which to begin. And really, we'd better. The job has to be tackled some day: and every day we put it off will make it harder to begin.

What, after all, is the alternative? You see clearly enough that nothing, not even God with all His power, can make 'X' really happy as long as 'X' remains envious, self-centered, and spiteful. Be sure there is something inside you which, unless it is altered, will put it out of God's power to prevent your being eternally miserable. While that something remains there can be no heaven for you, just as there can be no sweet smells for a man with a cold in the nose, and no music for a man who is deaf. It's not a question of God 'sending' us to Hell. In each of us there is something growing up which will of itself *be Hell* unless it is nipped in the bud. The matter is serious: let us put ourselves in His hands at once—this very day, this hour.

ON LIVING TODAY WHILE EXPECTING THE SECOND COMING TOMORROW

THE DOCTRINE OF the Second Coming teaches us that we do not and cannot know when the world drama will end. The curtain may be rung down at any moment: say, before you have finished reading this paragraph. This seems to some people intolerably frustrating. So many things would be interrupted. Perhaps you were going to get married next month, perhaps you were going to get a raise next week: you may be on the verge of a great scientific discov-

---

The World's Last Night, from the chapter titled "The World's Last Night."

ery; you may be maturing great social and political reforms. Surely no good and wise God would be so very unreasonable as to cut all this short? Not *now*, of all moments!

But we think thus because we keep on assuming that we know the play. We do not know the play. We do not even know whether we are in Act I or Act V. We do not know who are the major and who the minor characters. The Author knows. The audience, if there is an audience (if angels and archangels and all the company of heaven fill the pit and the stalls) may have an inkling. But we, never seeing the play from outside, never meeting any characters except the tiny minority who are 'on' in the same scenes as ourselves, wholly ignorant of the future and very imperfectly informed about the past, cannot tell at what moment the end ought to come. That it will come when it ought, we may be sure; but we waste our time in guessing when that will be. That it has a meaning we may be sure, but we cannot see it. When it is over, we may be told. We are led to expect that the Author will have something to say to each of us on the part that each of us has played. The playing it well is what matters infinitely.

The doctrine of the Second Coming, then, is not to be rejected because it conflicts with our favourite modern mythology. It is, for that very reason, to be the more valued and made more frequently the subject of meditation. It is the medicine our condition especially needs.

And with that, I turn to the practical. There is a real difficulty in giving this doctrine the place which it ought to have in our Christian life without, at the same time, running a certain risk. The fear of that risk probably deters many teachers who accept the doctrine from saying very much about it.

We must admit at once that this doctrine has, in the past, led Christians into very great follies. Apparently many people find it difficult to believe in this great event without trying to guess its date, or even without accepting as a certainty the date that any quack or hysteric offers them. To write a history of all these exploded predictions would need a book, and a sad, sordid, tragi-comical book it would be. One such prediction was circulating when St. Paul wrote his second letter to the Thessalonians. Someone had told them that 'the Day' was 'at hand'. This was apparently having the result which such predictions usually have: people were idling and playing the busybody. One of the most famous predictions was that of poor William Miller in 1843. Miller (whom I take to have been an honest fanatic) dated the Second Coming to the year, the day, and the very minute. A timely comet fostered the delusion. Thousands waited for the Lord at midnight on March 21st, and went home to a late breakfast on the 22nd followed by the jeers of a drunkard.

Clearly, no one wishes to say anything that will reawaken such mass hysteria. We must never speak to simple, excitable people about 'the Day' without emphasising again and again the utter impossibility of prediction. We must try to show them that that impossibility is an essential part of the doctrine. If you do not believe our Lord's words, why do you believe in His return at all? And if you do believe them must you not put away from you, utterly and forever, any hope of dating that return? His teaching on the subject quite clearly consisted of three propositions. (1) That He will certainly return. (2) That we cannot possibly find out when. (3) And that therefore we must always be ready for Him.

Note the *therefore*. Precisely because we cannot predict the moment, we must be ready at all moments. Our Lord repeated this practical conclusion again and again; as if the promise of the Return had been made for the sake of this conclusion alone. Watch, watch, is the burden of His advice. I shall come like a thief. You will not, I most solemnly assure you you will not, see Me approaching. If the householder had known at what time the burglar would arrive, he would have been ready for him. If the servant had known when his absent employer would come home, he would not have been found drunk in the kitchen. But they didn't. Nor will you. Therefore you must be ready at all times. The point is surely simple enough. The schoolboy does not know which part of his Virgil lesson he will be made to translate: that is why he must be prepared to translate *any* passage. The sentry does not know at what time an enemy will attack, or an officer inspect, his post: that is why he must keep awake *all* the time. The Return is wholly unpredictable. There will be wars and rumours of wars and all kinds of catastrophes, as there always are. Things will be, in that sense, normal, the hour before the heavens roll up like a scroll. You cannot guess it. If you could, one chief purpose for which it was foretold would be frustrated. And God's purposes are not so easily frustrated as that. One's ears should be closed against any future William Miller in advance. The folly of listening to him at all is almost equal to the folly of believing him. He *couldn't* know what he pretends, or thinks, he knows.

Of this folly George MacDonald has written well. 'Do those,' he asks, 'who say, Lo here or lo there are the signs of His coming, think to be too keen for

Him and spy His approach? When He tells them to watch lest He find them neglecting their work, they stare this way and that, and watch lest He should succeed in coming like a thief! Obedience is the one key of life.'

The doctrine of the Second Coming has failed, so far as we are concerned, if it does not make us realise that at every moment of every year in our lives Donne's question 'What if this present were the world's last night?' is equally relevant.

Sometimes this question has been pressed upon our minds with the purpose of exciting fear. I do not think that is its right use. I am, indeed, far from agreeing with those who think all religious fear barbarous and degrading and demand that it should be banished from the spiritual life. Perfect love, we know, casteth out fear. But so do several other things—ignorance, alcohol, passion, presumption, and stupidity. It is very desirable that we should all advance to that perfection of love in which we shall fear no longer; but it is very undesirable, until we have reached that stage, that we should allow any inferior agent to cast out our fear. The objection to any attempt at perpetual trepidation about the Second Coming is, in my view, quite a different one: namely, that it will certainly not succeed. Fear is an emotion: and it is quite impossible—even physically impossible—to maintain any emotion for very long. A perpetual excitement of hope about the Second Coming is impossible for the same reason. Crisis-feeling of any sort is essentially transitory. Feelings come and go, and when they come a good use can be made of them: they cannot be our regular spiritual diet.

What is important is not that we should always fear (or hope) about the End but that we should always remember, always take it into account. An analogy may here help. A man of seventy need not be always feeling (much less talking) about his approaching death: but a wise man of seventy should always take it into account. He would be foolish to embark on schemes which presuppose twenty more years of life: he would be criminally foolish not to make—

indeed, not to have made long since—his will. Now, what death is to each man, the Second Coming is to the whole human race. We all believe, I suppose, that a man should 'sit loose' to his own individual life, should remember how short, precarious, temporary, and provisional a thing it is; should never give all his heart to anything which will end when his life ends. What modern Christians find it harder to remember is that the whole life of humanity in this world is also precarious, temporary, provisional.

Any moralist will tell you that the personal triumph of an athlete or of a girl at a ball is transitory: the point is to remember that an empire or a civilisation is also transitory. All achievements and triumphs, insofar as they are merely this-worldly achievements and triumphs, will come to nothing in the end. Most scientists here join hands with the theologians; the earth will not always be habitable. Man, though longer-lived than men, is equally mortal. The difference is that whereas the scientists expect only a slow decay from within, we reckon with sudden interruption

from without—at any moment. ('What if this present were the world's last night?')

Taken by themselves, these considerations might
seem to invite a relaxation of our efforts for the good
of posterity: but if we remember that what may be
upon us at any moment is not merely an End but a
Judgment, they should have no such result. They
may, and should, correct the tendency of some mod-
erns to talk as though duties to posterity were the
only duties we had. I can imagine no man who will
look with more horror on the End than a conscien-
tious revolutionary who has, in a sense sincerely, been
justifying cruelties and injustices inflicted on millions
of his contemporaries by the benefits which he hopes
to confer on future generations: generations who, as
one terrible moment now reveals to him, were never
going to exist. Then he will see the massacres, the
faked trials, the deportations, to be all ineffaceably
real, an essential part, his part, in the drama that has
just ended: while the future Utopia had never been
anything but a fantasy.

Frantic administration of panaceas to the world is certainly discouraged by the reflection that 'this present' might be 'the world's last night'; sober work for the future, within the limits of ordinary morality and prudence, is not. For what comes is Judgment: happy are those whom it finds labouring in their vocations, whether they were merely going out to feed the pigs or laying good plans to deliver humanity a hundred years hence from some great evil. The curtain has indeed now fallen. Those pigs will never in fact be fed, the great campaign against White Slavery or Governmental Tyranny will never in fact proceed to victory. No matter; you were at your post when the Inspection came.

Our ancestors had a habit of using the word *Judgment* in this context as if it meant simply 'punishment': hence the popular expression, 'It's a judgment on him.' I believe we can sometimes render the thing more vivid to ourselves by taking judgment in a stricter sense: not as the sentence or award, but as the Verdict. Some day (and 'What if this present were the world's last night?') an absolutely correct verdict—if you like, a perfect critique—will be passed on what each of us is.

We have all encountered judgments or verdicts on ourselves in this life. Every now and then we discover what our fellow creatures really think of us. I don't of course mean what they tell us to our faces: that we usually have to discount. I am thinking of what we sometimes overhear by accident or of the opinions about us which our neighbours or employees or subordinates unknowingly reveal in their actions: and of the terrible, or lovely, judgments artlessly betrayed by children or even animals. Such discoveries can be the bitterest or sweetest experiences we have. But of course both the bitter and the sweet are limited by our doubt as to the wisdom of those who judge. We always hope that those who so clearly think us cowards or bullies are ignorant and malicious; we always fear that those who trust us or admire us are misled by partiality. I suppose the experience of the Final Judgment (which may break in upon us at any moment) will be like these little experiences, but magnified to the Nth.

For it will be infallible judgment. If it is favourable we shall have no fear, if unfavourable, no hope, that it is wrong. We shall not only believe, we shall know, know beyond doubt in every fibre of our appalled or delighted being, that as the Judge has said, so we are: neither more nor less nor other. We shall perhaps even realise that in some dim fashion we could have known it all along. We shall know and all creation will know too: our ancestors, our parents, our wives or husbands, our children. The unanswerable and (by then) self-evident truth about each will be known to all.

I do not find that pictures of physical catastrophe—that sign in the clouds, those heavens rolled up like a scroll—help one so much as the naked idea of Judgment. We cannot always be excited. We can, perhaps, train ourselves to ask more and more often how the thing which we are saying or doing (or failing to do) at each moment will look when the irresistible light streams in upon it; that light which is so different from the light of this world—and yet, even now, we know just enough of it to take it into account. Women sometimes have the problem of trying to judge by artificial light how a dress will look by daylight. That is very like the problem of all of us: to dress our souls not for the electric lights of the present world but for the daylight of the next. The good dress is the one that will face that light. For that light will last longer.

ON FORGIVENESS AS A
NECESSARY PRACTICE

WE SAY A great many things in church (and out of church too) without thinking of what we are saying. For instance, we say in the Creed "I believe in the forgiveness of sins." I had been saying it for several years before I asked myself why it was in the Creed. At first sight it seems hardly worth putting in. "If one is a Christian," I thought, "of course one believes in the forgiveness of sins. It goes without saying." But the people who compiled the Creed apparently thought that this was a part of our belief which we needed to be reminded of every time we went to church. And I

The Weight of Glory, from the chapter titled "On Forgiveness."

have begun to see that, as far as I am concerned, they were right. To believe in the forgiveness of sins is not nearly so easy as I thought. Real belief in it is the sort of thing that very easily slips away if we don't keep on polishing it up.

We believe that God forgives us our sins; but also that He will not do so unless we forgive other people their sins against us. There is no doubt about the second part of this statement. It is in the Lord's Prayer; it was emphatically stated by our Lord. If you don't forgive you will not be forgiven. No part of His teaching is clearer, and there are no exceptions to it. He doesn't say that we are to forgive other people's sins provided they are not too frightful, or provided there are extenuating circumstances, or anything of that sort. We are to forgive them all, however spiteful, however mean, however often they are repeated. If we don't, we shall be forgiven none of our own.

Now it seems to me that we often make a mistake both about God's forgiveness of our sins and about the forgiveness we are told to offer to other people's sins. Take it first about God's forgiveness. I find that when I think I am asking God to forgive me I am often in reality (unless I watch myself very carefully) asking Him to do something quite different. I am asking Him not to forgive me but to excuse me. But there is all the difference in the world between forgiving and excusing. Forgiveness says "Yes, you have done this thing, but I accept your apology; I will never hold it against you and everything between us two will be exactly as it was before." But excusing says "I see that you couldn't help it or didn't mean it; you weren't really to blame." If one was not really to blame then there is nothing to forgive. In that sense forgiveness and excusing are almost opposites. Of course, in dozens of cases, either between God and man, or between one man and another, there may be a mixture of the two. Part of what seemed at first to be the sins turns out to be really nobody's fault and is excused; the bit that is left over is forgiven. If you had a perfect excuse, you would not need forgiveness; if the whole of your action needs forgiveness, then there was no excuse for it. But the trouble is that what we call "asking God's forgiveness" very often really consists in asking God to accept our excuses. What leads us into this mistake is the fact that there usually is some amount of excuse, some "extenuating circumstances." We are so very anxious to point these out to God (and to ourselves) that we are apt to forget the really important thing; that is, the bit left over, the bit which the excuses don't cover, the bit which is inexcusable but not, thank God, unforgivable. And if we forget this, we shall go away imagining that we have repented and been forgiven when all that has really happened is that we have satisfied ourselves with our own excuses. They may be very bad excuses; we are all too easily satisfied about ourselves.

There are two remedies for this danger. One is to remember that God knows all the real excuses very much better than we do. If there are real "extenuating circumstances" there is no fear that He will overlook them. Often He must know many excuses that we have never thought of, and therefore humble souls will, after death, have the delightful surprise of discovering that on certain occasions they sinned much less than they had thought. All the real excusing He will do. What we have got to take to Him is the inexcusable bit, the sin. We are only wasting time by talking about all the parts which can (we think) be excused. When you go to a doctor you show him the bit of you that is wrong—say, a broken arm. It would be a mere waste of time to keep on explaining that your legs and eyes and throat are all right. You may be mistaken in thinking so, and anyway, if they are really all right, the doctor will know that.

The second remedy is really and truly to believe in the forgiveness of sins. A great deal of our anxiety to make excuses comes from not really believing in it, from thinking that God will not take us to Himself again unless He is satisfied that some sort of case can be made out in our favour. But that would not be forgiveness at all. Real forgiveness means looking steadily at the sin, the sin that is left over without any excuse, after all allowances have been made, and seeing it in all its horror, dirt, meanness, and malice, and nevertheless being wholly reconciled to the man who has done it. That, and only that, is forgiveness, and that we can always have from God if we ask for it.

When it comes to a question of our forgiving other people, it is partly the same and partly different. It is the same because, here also, forgiving does not mean excusing. Many people seem to think it does. They think that if you ask them to forgive someone who has cheated or bullied them you are trying to make out that there was really no cheating or no bullying. But if that were so, there would be nothing to forgive. They keep on replying, "But I tell you the man broke a most solemn promise." Exactly: that is precisely what you have to forgive. (This doesn't mean that you must necessarily believe his next promise. It does mean that you must make every effort to kill every taste of resentment in your own heart—every wish to humiliate or hurt him or to pay him out.) The difference between this situation and the one in which you are asking God's forgiveness is this. In our own case we accept excuses too easily; in other people's we do not accept them easily enough. As regards my own sins it is a safe bet (though not a certainty) that the excuses are not really so good as I think; as regards other men's sins against me it is a safe bet (though not a certainty) that the excuses are better than I think. One must therefore begin by attending to everything which may show that the other man was not so much to blame as we thought. But even if he is absolutely fully to blame we still have to forgive him; and even if ninety-nine per cent of his apparent guilt can be explained away by really good excuses, the problem of forgiveness begins with the one per cent of guilt which is left over. To excuse what can really produce good excuses is not Christian charity; it is only fairness. To be a Christian means to forgive the inexcusable, because God has forgiven the inexcusable in you.

This is hard. It is perhaps not so hard to forgive a single great injury. But to forgive the incessant provocations of daily life—to keep on forgiving the bossy mother-in-law, the bullying husband, the nagging wife, the selfish daughter, the deceitful son—how can we do it? Only, I think, by remembering where we stand, by meaning our words when we say in our prayers each night "forgive us our trespasses as we forgive those that trespass against us." We are offered forgiveness on no other terms. To refuse it is to refuse God's mercy for ourselves. There is no hint of exceptions and God means what He says.

ON DENYING ONESELF
WHILE LOVING ONESELF

SELF-RENUNCIATION IS THOUGHT to be, and indeed is, very near the core of Christian ethics. When Aristotle writes in praise of a certain kind of self-love, we may feel, despite the careful distinctions which he draws between the legitimate and the illegitimate *Philautia*,[1] that here we strike something essentially sub-Christian. It is more difficult, however, to decide what we think of St. François de Sales's chapter, *De la douceur envers nous-mêsmes*,[2] where we are forbidden to indulge resentment even against ourselves and

---

God in the Dock, from the chapter titled
"Two Ways with the Self."

advised to reprove even our own faults *avec des remonstrances douces et tranquilles*,[3] feeling more com-
passion than passion. In the same spirit, Lady Julian
of Norwich would have us 'loving and peaceable,' not
only to our 'even-Christians,' but to 'ourself.'[4] Even
the New Testament bids me love my neighbour 'as
myself,'[5] which would be a horrible command if the
self were simply to be hated. Yet our Lord also says
that a true disciple must 'hate his own life.'[6]

We must not explain this apparent contradiction by
saying that self-love is right up to a certain point and
wrong beyond that point. The question is not one of
degree. There are two kinds of self-hatred which look
rather alike in their earlier stages, but of which one
is wrong from the beginning and the other right to
the end. When Shelley speaks of self-contempt as the
source of cruelty, or when a later poet says that he has
no stomach for the man 'who loathes his neighbour as
himself,' they are referring to a very real and very un-
Christian hatred of the self which may make diaboli-
cal a man whom common selfishness would have left

(at least, for a while) merely animal. The hard-boiled economist or psychologist of our own day, recognizing the 'ideological taint' or Freudian motive in his own make-up, does not necessarily learn Christian humility. He may end in what is called a 'low view' of all souls, including his own, which expresses itself in cynicism or cruelty, or both. Even Christians, if they accept in certain forms the doctrine of total depravity, are not always free from the danger. The logical conclusion of the process is the worship of suffering—for others as well as for the self—which we see, if I read it aright, in Mr. David Lindsay's *Voyage to Arcturus*, or that extraordinary vacancy which Shakespeare depicts at the end of *Richard III*. Richard in his agony tries to turn to self-love. But he has been 'seeing through' all emotions so long that he 'sees through' even this. It becomes a mere tautology: 'Richard loves Richard; that is, I am I.'[7]

Now, the self can be regarded in two ways. On the one hand, it is God's creature, an occasion of love and rejoicing; now, indeed, hateful in condition, but to be pitied and healed. On the other hand, it is that one self of all others which is called *I* and *me*, and which on that ground puts forward an irrational claim to preference. This claim is to be not only hated, but simply killed; 'never,' as George MacDonald says, 'to be allowed a moment's respite from eternal death.' The Christian must wage endless war against the clamor of the *ego* as *ego*: but he loves and approves selves as such, though not their sins. The very self-love which he has to reject is to him a specimen of how he ought to feel to all selves; and he may hope that when he has truly learned (which will hardly be in this life) to love his neighbour as himself, he may then be able to love himself as his neighbour: that is, with charity instead of partiality. The other kind of self-hatred, on the contrary, hates selves as such. It begins by accepting the special value of the particular self called *me*; then, wounded in its pride to find that such a darling object should be so disappointing, it seeks revenge, first upon that self, then on all. Deeply egoistic, but now with an inverted egoism, it uses the revealing argument, 'I don't spare myself'—with the implication 'then *a fortiori* I need not spare others'—and becomes like the centurion in Tacitus, "*immitior quia toleraverat.*"[8]

The wrong asceticism torments the self: the right kind Kills the selfness. We must die daily: but it is better to love the self than to love nothing, and to pity the self than to pity no one.

---

[1] *Nicomachean Ethics*, bk. 9, ch. 8.

[2] Pt. III, ch. 9 'Of Meekness towards Ourselves' in the *Introduction to the Devout Life* (Lyons, 1609).

[3] 'with mild and calm remonstrances'.

[4] *The Sixteen Revelations of Divine Love*, ch. 49.

[5] Matthew 19:19, 22, 39; Mark 12:31, 33; Romans 13:9; Galatians v. 14; James 2:8.

[6] Luke 14:26; John 12:25.

[7] *Richard III*, V, iii, 184.

[8] *Annals*, Bk. 1, sect. 20, line 14. 'More relentless because he had endured (it himself).'

ON DOUBTS AND THE
GIFT OF FAITH

IN GENERAL WE are shy of speaking plain about Faith as a virtue. It looks so like praising an intention to believe what you want to believe in the face of evidence to the contrary: the American in the old story defined Faith as 'the power of believing what we know to be untrue'. Now I define Faith as the power of continuing to believe what we once honestly thought to be true until cogent reasons for honestly changing our minds are brought before us. The difficulty of such continuing to believe is constantly

Christian Reflections, from the chapter titled
"Religion: Reality or Substitute?"

ignored or misunderstood in discussions of this subject. It is always assumed that the difficulties of faith
are intellectual difficulties, that a man who has once
accepted a certain proposition will automatically go
on believing it till real grounds for disbelief occur.
Nothing could be more superficial. How many of
the freshmen who come up to Oxford from religious
homes and lose their Christianity in the first year have
been honestly *argued* out of it? How many of our
own sudden temporary losses of faith have a rational
basis which would stand examination for a moment? I
don't know how it is with others, but I find that mere
change of scene always has a tendency to decrease my
faith at first—God is less credible when I pray in a
hotel bedroom than when I am in college. The society of unbelievers makes Faith harder even when they
are people whose opinions, on any other subject, are
known to be worthless.

These irrational fluctuations in belief are not pecu-
liar to religious belief. They are happening about all
our beliefs all day long. Haven't you noticed it with

our thoughts about the war? Some days, of course, there is really good or really bad news, which gives us rational grounds for increased optimism or pessimism. But everyone must have experienced days in which we are caught up in a great wave of confidence or down into a trough of anxiety though there are no new grounds either for the one or the other. Of course, once the mood is on us, we *find* reasons soon enough. We say that we've been 'thinking it over': but it is pretty plain that the mood has created the reasons and not *vice versa*. But there are examples closer to the Christian problem even than these. There are things, say in learning to swim or to climb, which look dangerous and aren't. Your instructor tells you it's safe. You have good reason from past experience to trust him. Perhaps you can even see for yourself, by your own reason, that it is safe. But the crucial question is, will you be able to go on believing this when you actually see the cliff edge below you or actually feel yourself unsupported in the water? You will have no *rational* grounds for disbelieving. It is your senses and your imagination that are going to attack belief. Here, as in the New Testament, the conflict is not between faith and reason but between faith and sight. We can face things which we *know* to be dangerous if they don't look or sound too dangerous; our real trouble is often with things we *know* to be safe but which look dreadful. Our faith in Christ wavers not so much when real arguments come against it as when it *looks* improbable—when the whole world takes on that desolate *look* which really tells us much more about the state of our passions and even our digestion than about reality.

When we exhort people to Faith as a virtue, to the settled intention of continuing to believe certain things, we are not exhorting them to fight against reason. The intention of continuing to believe is required because, though Reason is divine, human reasoners are not. When once passion takes part in the game, the human reason, unassisted by Grace, has about as much chance of retaining its hold on truths already gained as a snowflake has of retaining its consistency in the mouth of a blast furnace. The sort of arguments against Christianity which our reason can be persuaded to accept at the moment of yielding to temptation are often preposterous. Reason may win truths; without Faith she will retain them just so long as Satan pleases. There is nothing we cannot be made to believe or disbelieve. If we wish to be rational, not now and then, but constantly, we must pray for the gift of Faith, for the power to go on believing not in the teeth of reason but in the teeth of lust and terror and jealousy and boredom and indifference that which reason, authority, or experience, or all three, have once delivered to us for truth. And the answer to that prayer will, perhaps, surprise us when it comes. For I am not sure, after all, whether one of the causes of our weak faith is not a secret wish that our faith should *not* be very strong. Is there some reservation in our minds? Some fear of what it might be like if our religion became *quite* real? I hope not. God help us all, and forgive us.

ON THE APPEAL AND
CHALLENGES OF HOME LIFE

'SO,' SAID THE preacher, 'the home must be the foundation of our national life. It is there, all said and done, that character is formed. It is there that we appear as we really are. It is there we can fling aside the weary disguises of the outer world and be ourselves. It is there that we retreat from the noise and stress and temptation and dissipation of daily life to seek the sources of fresh strength and renewed purity...' And as he spoke I noticed that all confidence in him had departed from every member of that congregation

God in the Dock, from the chapter titled
"The Sermon and the Lunch."

who was under thirty. They had been listening well up to this point. Now the shufflings and coughings began. Pews creaked; muscles relaxed. The sermon, for all practical purposes, was over; the five minutes for which the preacher continued talking were a total waste of time—at least for most of us.

Whether I wasted them or not is for you to judge. I certainly did not hear any more of the sermon. I was thinking; and the starting point of my thought was the question, 'How can he? How can *he* of all people?' For I knew the preacher's own home pretty well. In fact, I had been lunching there that very day, making a fifth to the Vicar and the Vicar's wife and the son (R.A.F.)[1] and the daughter (A.T.S.),[2] who happened both to be on leave. I could have avoided it, but the girl had whispered to me, 'For God's sake stay to lunch if they ask you. It's always a little less frightful when there's a visitor.'

Lunch at the vicarage nearly always follows the same pattern. It starts with a desperate attempt on the part of the young people to keep up a bright patter of trivial conversation: trivial not because they are trivially minded (you can have real conversation with them if you get them alone), but because it would never occur to either of them to say at home anything they were really thinking, unless it is forced out of them by anger. They are talking only to try to keep their parents quiet. They fail. The Vicar, ruthlessly interrupting, cuts in on a quite different subject. He is telling us how to re-educate Germany. He has never been there and seems to know nothing either of German history or the German language. 'But, father', begins the son, and gets no further. His mother is now talking, though nobody knows exactly when she began. She is in the middle of a complicated story about how badly some neighbour has treated her. Though it goes on a long time, we never learn either how it began or how it ended: it is all middle. 'Mother, that's not quite fair,' says the daughter at last. 'Mrs. Walker never said—' but her father's voice booms in again. He is telling his son about the organization of the R.A.F. So it goes on until either the Vicar or his wife says something so preposterous that the boy or the girl contradicts and insists on making the contradiction heard. The real minds of the young people have at last been called into action. They talk fiercely, quickly, contemptuously. They have facts and logic on their side. There is an answering flare-up from the parents. The father storms; the mother is (oh, blessed domestic queen's move!) 'hurt'—plays pathos for all she is worth. The daughter becomes ironical. The father and son, elaborately ignoring each other, start talking to me. The lunch party is in ruins.

The memory of that lunch worries me during the last few minutes of the sermon. I am not worried by the fact that the Vicar's practise differs from his precept. That is, no doubt, regrettable, but it is nothing to the purpose. As Dr. Johnson said, precept may be very sincere (and, let us add, very profitable) where practice is very imperfect,[3] and no one but a fool would discount a doctor's warnings about alcoholic poisoning because the doctor himself drank too much. What worries me is the fact that the Vicar is not telling us at all that home life is difficult and has, like every form of life, its own proper temptations and corruptions. He keeps on talking as if 'home' were a panacea, a magical charm which of itself was bound to produce happiness and virtue. The trouble is not that he is insincere but that he is a fool. He is not talking from his own experience of family life at all: he is automatically reproducing a sentimental tradition—and it happens to be a false tradition. That is why the congregation have stopped listening to him.

If Christian teachers wish to recall Christian people to domesticity—and I, for one, believe that people must be recalled to it—the first necessity is to stop telling lies about home life and to substitute realistic teaching. Perhaps the fundamental principles would be something like this:

1. Since the Fall no organization or way of life whatever has a natural tendency to go right. In the Middle Ages some people thought that if only they entered a religious order they would find themselves automatically becoming holy and happy: the whole

native literature of the period echoes with the exposure of that fatal error. In the nineteenth century some people thought that monogamous family life would automatically make them holy and happy; the savage anti-domestic literature of modern times—the Samuel Butlers, the Gosses, the Shaws—delivered the answer. In both cases the 'debunkers' may have been wrong about principles and may have forgotten the maxim *abusus non tollit usum*:[4] but in both cases they were pretty right about matter of fact. Both family life and monastic life were often detestable, and it should be noticed that the serious defenders of both are well aware of the dangers and free of the sentimental illusion. The author of the *Imitation of Christ* knows (no one better) how easily monastic life goes wrong. Charlotte M. Yonge makes it abundantly clear that domesticity is no passport to heaven on earth but an arduous vocation—a sea full of hidden rocks and perilous ice shores only to be navigated by one who uses a celestial chart. That is the first point on which we must be absolutely clear. The family, like the nation, can be offered to God, can be converted and redeemed, and will then become the channel of particular blessings and graces. But, like everything else that is human, it needs redemption. Unredeemed, it will produce only particular temptations, corruptions, and miseries. Charity begins at home: so does uncharity.

2. By the conversion or sanctification of family life we must be careful to mean something more than the preservation of 'love' in the sense of natural affection. Love (in that sense) is not enough. Affection, as distinct from charity, is not a cause of lasting happiness. Left to its natural bent affection becomes in the end greedy, naggingly solicitous, jealous, exacting, timorous. It suffers agony when its object is absent— but is not repaid by any long enjoyment when the object is present. Even at the Vicar's lunch table affection was partly the cause of the quarrel. That son would have borne patiently and humorously from any other old man the silliness which enraged him in his father. It is because he still (in some fashion)

'cares' that he is impatient. The Vicar's wife would not be quite that endless whimper of self-pity which she now is if she did not (in a sense) 'love' the family: the continued disappointment of her continued and ruthless demand for sympathy, for affection, for appreciation has helped to make her what she is. I do not think this aspect of affection is nearly enough noticed by most popular moralists. The greed to be loved is a fearful thing. Some of those who say (and almost with pride) that they live only for love come, at last, to live in incessant resentment.

3. We must realise the yawning pitfall in that very characteristic of home life which is so often glibly paraded as its principal attraction. 'It is there that we appear as we really are: it is there that we can fling aside the disguises and be ourselves.' These words, in the Vicar's mouth, were only too true and he showed at the lunch table what they meant. Outside his own house he behaves with ordinary courtesy. He would not have interrupted any other young man as he interrupted his son. He would not, in any other soci-

ety, have talked confident nonsense about subjects of which he was totally ignorant: or, if he had, he would have accepted correction with good temper. In fact, he values home as the place where he can 'be himself' in the sense of trampling on all the restraints which civilized humanity has found indispensable for tolerable social intercourse. And this, I think, is very common. What chiefly distinguishes domestic from public conversation is surely very often simply its downright rudeness. What distinguishes domestic behaviour is often its selfishness, slovenliness, incivility—even brutality. And it will often happen that those who praise home life most loudly are the worst offenders in this respect: they praise it—they are always glad to get home, hate the outer world, can't stand visitors, can't be bothered meeting people, etc.—because the freedoms in which they indulge themselves at home have ended by making them unfit for civilized society. If they practised elsewhere the only behaviour they now find 'natural' they would simply be knocked down.

4. How, then, *are* people to behave at home? If a man can't be comfortable and unguarded, can't take his ease and 'be himself' in his own house, where can he? That is, I confess, the trouble. The answer is an alarming one. There is *nowhere* this side of heaven where one can safely lay the reins on the horse's neck. It will never be lawful simply to 'be ourselves' until 'ourselves' have become sons of God. It is all there in the hymn—'Christian, seek not yet repose.' This does not mean, of course, that there is no difference between home life and general society. It does mean that home life has its own rule of courtesy—a code more intimate, more subtle, more sensitive, and, therefore, in some ways more difficult, than that of the outer world.

5. Finally, must we not teach that if the home is to be a means of grace it must be a place of *rules*? There cannot be a common life without a *regula*. The alternative to rule is not freedom but the unconstitutional (and often unconscious) tyranny of the most selfish member.

In a word, must we not either cease to preach domesticity or else begin to preach it seriously? Must we not abandon sentimental eulogies and begin to give practical advice on the high, hard, lovely, and adventurous art of really creating the Christian family?

[1] Royal Air Force.

[2] Auxiliary Territorial Service.

[3] James Boswell, *Life of Johnson*, ed. George Birkbeck Hill (Oxford, 1934), vol. IV, p. 397 (2 December 1784).

[4] 'The abuse does not abolish the use.'

ON HOW WE SPREAD THE CHRIST-LIFE WITHIN

THE PERFECT SURRENDER and humiliation were undergone by Christ: perfect because He was God, surrender and humiliation because He was man. Now the Christian belief is that if we somehow share the humility and suffering of Christ we shall also share in His conquest of death and find a new life after we have died and in it become perfect, and perfectly happy, creatures. This means something much more than our trying to follow His teaching. People often ask when the next step in evolution—the step to some-

---

Mere Christianity, from the chapter titled
"The Practical Conclusion."

thing beyond man—will happen. But in the Christian view, it has happened already. In Christ a new kind of man appeared: and the new kind of life which began in Him is to be put into us.

How is this to be done? Now, please remember how we acquired the old, ordinary kind of life. We derived it from others, from our father and mother and all our ancestors, without our consent—and by a very curious process, involving pleasure, pain, and danger. A process you would never have guessed. Most of us spend a good many years in childhood trying to guess it: and some children, when they are first told, do not believe it—and I am not sure that I blame them, for it is very odd. Now the God who arranged that process is the same God who arranges how the new kind of life—the Christ-life—is to be spread. We must be prepared for it being odd too. He did not consult us when He invented sex: He has not consulted us either when He invented this.

There are three things that spread the Christ-life to us: baptism, belief, and that mysterious action which different Christians call by different names—Holy Communion, the Mass, the Lord's Supper. At least, those are the three ordinary methods. I am not saying there may not be special cases where it is spread without one or more of these. I have not time to go into special cases, and I do not know enough. If you are trying in a few minutes to tell a man how to get to Edinburgh you will tell him the trains: he can, it is true, get there by boat or by a plane, but you will hardly bring that in. And I am not saying anything about which of these three things is the most essential. My Methodist friend would like me to say more about belief and less (in proportion) about the other two. But I am not going into that. Anyone who professes to teach you Christian doctrine will, in fact, tell you to use all three, and that is enough for our present purpose.

I cannot myself see why these things should be the conductors of the new kind of life. But then, if one did not happen to know, I should never have seen any connection between a particular physical pleasure and the appearance of a new human being in the world. We have to take reality as it comes to us: there is no good jabbering about what it ought to be like or what we should have expected it to be like. But though I cannot see why it should be so, I can tell you why I believe it is so. I have explained why I have to believe that Jesus was (and is) God. And it seems plain as a matter of history that He taught His followers that the new life was communicated in this way. In other words, I believe it on His authority. Do not be scared by the word authority. Believing things on authority only means believing them because you have been told them by someone you think trustworthy. Ninety-nine percent of the things you believe are believed on authority. I believe there is such a place as New York. I have not seen it myself. I could not prove by abstract reasoning that there must be such a place. I believe it because reliable people have told me so. The ordinary man believes in the Solar System, atoms, evolution, and the circulation of the blood on authority—because the scientists say so. Every his-

torical statement in the world is believed on authority. None of us has seen the Norman Conquest or the
defeat of the Armada. None of us could prove them
by pure logic as you prove a thing in mathematics.
We believe them simply because people who did see
them have left writings that tell us about them: in fact,
on authority. A man who jibbed at authority in other
things as some people do in religion would have to be
content to know nothing all his life.

Do not think I am setting up baptism and belief and
the Holy Communion as things that will do instead of
your own attempts to copy Christ. Your natural life is
derived from your parents; that does not mean it will
stay there if you do nothing about it. You can lose it
by neglect, or you can drive it away by committing
suicide. You have to feed it and look after it: but always remember you are not making it, you are only
keeping up a life you got from someone else. In the
same way a Christian can lose the Christ-life which
has been put into him, and he has to make efforts to
keep it. But even the best Christian that ever lived is

not acting on his own steam—he is only nourishing or protecting a life he could never have acquired by his own efforts. And that has practical consequences. As long as the natural life is in your body, it will do a lot towards repairing that body. Cut it, and up to a point it will heal, as a dead body would not. A live body is not one that never gets hurt, but one that can to some extent repair itself. In the same way a Christian is not a man who never goes wrong, but a man who is enabled to repent and pick himself up and begin over again after each stumble—because the Christ-life is inside him, repairing him all the time, enabling him to repeat (in some degree) the kind of voluntary death which Christ Himself carried out.

That is why the Christian is in a different position from other people who are trying to be good. They hope, by being good, to please God if there is one; or—if they think there is not—at least they hope to deserve approval from good men. But the Christian thinks any good he does comes from the Christ-life inside him. He does not think God will love us because we are good, but that God will make us good because He loves us; just as the roof of a greenhouse does not attract the sun because it is bright, but becomes bright because the sun shines on it.

And let me make it quite clear that when Christians say the Christ-life is in them, they do not mean simply something mental or moral. When they speak of being 'in Christ' or of Christ being 'in them', this is not simply a way of saying that they are thinking about Christ or copying Him. They mean that Christ is actually operating through them; that the whole mass of Christians are the physical organism through which Christ acts—that we are His fingers and muscles, the cells of His body. And perhaps that explains one or two things. It explains why this new life is spread not only by purely mental acts like belief, but by bodily acts like baptism and Holy Communion. It is not merely the spreading of an idea; it is more like evolution—a biological or superbiological fact. There is no good trying to be more spiritual than God. God never meant man to be a purely spiritual creature. That is why He uses material things like bread and wine to put the new life into us. We may think this rather crude and unspiritual. God does not: He invented eating. He likes matter. He invented it.

Here is another thing that used to puzzle me. Is it not frightfully unfair that this new life should be confined to people who have heard of Christ and been able to believe in Him? But the truth is God has not told us what His arrangements about the other people are. We do know that no man can be saved except through Christ; we do not know that only those who know Him can be saved through Him. But in the meantime, if you are worried about the people outside, the most unreasonable thing you can do is to remain outside yourself. Christians are Christ's body, the organism through which He works. Every addition to that body enables Him to do more. If you want to help those outside you must add your own little cell to the body of Christ who alone can help them. Cutting off a man's fingers would be an odd way of getting him to do more work.

Another possible objection is this. Why is God landing in this enemy-occupied world in disguise and starting a sort of secret society to undermine the devil? Why is He not landing in force, invading it? Is it that He is not strong enough? Well, Christians think He is going to land in force; we do not know when. But we can guess why He is delaying. He wants to give us the chance of joining His side freely. I do not suppose you and I would have thought much of a Frenchman who waited till the Allies were marching into Germany and then announced he was on our side. God will invade. But I wonder whether people who ask God to interfere openly and directly in our world quite realise what it will be like when He does. When that happens, it is the end of the world. When the author walks on to the stage the play is over. God is going to invade, all right: but what is the good of saying you are on His side then, when you see the whole natural universe melting away like a dream and something else—something it never entered your head to conceive—comes crashing in; something so beautiful to some of us and so terrible to others that none of us will have any choice left? For this time it will be God without disguise; something so overwhelming that it will strike either irresistible love or irresistible horror into every creature. It will be too late then to choose your side. There is no use saying you choose to lie down when it has become impossible to stand up. That will not be the time for choosing: it will be the time when we discover which side we really have chosen, whether we realised it before or not. Now, to-day, this moment, is our chance to choose the right side. God is holding back to give us that chance. It will not last forever. We must take it or leave it.

ON WHAT IT MEANS TO SAY, "TO LIVE IS CHRIST"

THERE ARE THREE kinds of people in the world. The first class is of those who live simply for their own sake and pleasure, regarding Man and Nature as so much raw material to be cut up into whatever shape may serve them. In the second class are those who acknowledge some other claim upon them—the will of God, the categorical imperative, or the good of society—and honestly try to pursue their own interests no further than this claim will allow. They try to surrender to the higher claim as much as it demands, like men paying a tax, but hope, like other taxpayers,

Present Concerns, from the chapter titled "Three Kinds of Men."

that what is left over will be enough for them to live on. Their life is divided, like a soldier's or a school-boy's life, into time 'on parade' and 'off parade', 'in school' and 'out of school'. But the third class is of those who can say like St. Paul that for them 'to live is Christ'.[1] These people have got rid of the tiresome business of adjusting the rival claims of Self and God by the simple expedient of rejecting the claims of Self altogether. The old egoistic will has been turned round, reconditioned, and made into a new thing. The will of Christ no longer limits theirs; it is theirs. All their time, in belonging to Him, belongs also to them, for they are His.

And because there are three classes, any merely twofold division of the world into good and bad is disastrous. It overlooks the fact that the members of the second class (to which most of us belong) are always and necessarily unhappy. The tax which moral conscience levies on our desires does not in fact leave us enough to live on. As long as we are in this class we must either feel guilt because we have not paid the tax or penury because we have. The Christian doctrine that there is no 'salvation' by works done according to the moral law is a fact of daily experience. Back or on we must go. But there is no going on simply by our own efforts. If the new Self, the new Will, does not come at His own good pleasure to be born in us, we cannot produce Him synthetically.

The price of Christ is something, in a way, much easier than moral effort—it is to want Him. It is true that the wanting itself would be beyond our power but for one fact. The world is so built that, to help us desert our own satisfactions, they desert us. War and trouble and finally old age take from us one by one all those things that the natural Self hoped for at its setting out. Begging is our only wisdom, and want in the end makes it easier for us to be beggars. Even on those terms the Mercy will receive us.

[1] Philippians 1:21.

ON THE CHRISTIAN ART
OF ATTAINING GLORY

IF YOU ASKED twenty good men today what they thought the highest of the virtues, nineteen of them would reply, Unselfishness. But if you had asked almost any of the great Christians of old, he would have replied, Love. You see what has happened? A negative term has been substituted for a positive, and this is of more than philological importance. The negative idea of Unselfishness carries with it the suggestion not primarily of securing good things for others, but of going without them ourselves, as if our abstinence

---

The Weight of Glory, from the chapter titled
"The Weight of Glory."

and not their happiness was the important point. I do not think this is the Christian virtue of Love. The New Testament has lots to say about self-denial, but not about self-denial as an end in itself. We are told to deny ourselves and to take up our crosses in order that we may follow Christ; and nearly every description of what we shall ultimately find if we do so contains an appeal to desire. If there lurks in most modern minds the notion that to desire our own good and earnestly to hope for the enjoyment of it is a bad thing, I submit that this notion has crept in from Kant and the Stoics and is no part of the Christian faith. Indeed, if we consider the unblushing promises of reward and the staggering nature of the rewards promised in the Gospels, it would seem that Our Lord finds our desires not too strong, but too weak. We are half-hearted creatures, fooling about with drink and sex and ambition when infinite joy is offered us, like an ignorant child who wants to go on making mud pies in a slum because he cannot imagine what is meant by the offer of a holiday at the sea. We are far too easily pleased.

We must not be troubled by unbelievers when they say that this promise of reward makes the Christian life a mercenary affair. There are different kinds of rewards. There is the reward which has no natural connection with the things you do to earn it and is quite foreign to the desires that ought to accompany those things. Money is not the natural reward of love; that is why we call a man mercenary if he marries a woman for the sake of her money. But marriage is the proper reward for a real lover, and he is not mercenary for desiring it. A general who fights well in order to get a peerage is mercenary; a general who fights for victory is not, victory being the proper reward of battle as marriage is the proper reward of love. The proper rewards are not simply tacked on to the activity for which they are given, but are the activity itself in consummation. There is also a third case, which is more complicated. An enjoyment of Greek poetry is certainly a proper, and not a mercenary, reward for learning Greek; but only those who have reached the stage of enjoying Greek poetry can tell from their own experience that this is so. The schoolboy beginning Greek grammar cannot look forward to his adult enjoyment of Sophocles as a lover looks forward to marriage or a general to victory. He has to begin by working for marks, or to escape punishment, or to please his parents, or, at best, in the hope of a future good which he cannot at present imagine or desire. His position, therefore, bears a certain resemblance to that of the mercenary; the reward he is going to get will, in actual fact, be a natural or proper reward, but he will not know that till he has got it. Of course, he gets it gradually; enjoyment creeps in upon the mere drudgery, and nobody could point to a day or an hour when the one ceased and the other began. But it is just insofar as he approaches the reward that he becomes able to desire it for its own sake; indeed, the power of so desiring it is itself a preliminary reward.

The Christian, in relation to heaven, is in much the same position as this schoolboy. Those who have attained everlasting life in the vision of God doubtless know very well that it is no mere bribe, but the very consummation of their earthly discipleship; but we who have not yet attained it cannot know this in the same way, and cannot even begin to know it at all except by continuing to obey and finding the first reward of our obedience in our increasing power to desire the ultimate reward. Just in proportion as the desire grows, our fear lest it should be a mercenary desire will die away and finally be recognised as an absurdity. But probably this will not, for most of us, happen in a day; poetry replaces grammar, gospel replaces law, longing transforms obedience, as gradually as the tide lifts a grounded ship.

But there is one other important similarity between the schoolboy and ourselves. If he is an imaginative boy, he will, quite probably, be revelling in the English poets and romancers suitable to his age some time before he begins to suspect that Greek grammar is going to lead him to more and more enjoyments of this same sort. He may even be neglecting his Greek to read Shelley and Swinburne in secret. In other words, the desire which Greek is really going to gratify already exists in him and is attached to objects which seem to him quite unconnected with Xenophon and the verbs in Greek. Now, if we are made for heaven, the desire for our proper place will be already in us, but not yet attached to the true object, and will even appear as the rival of that object. And this, I think, is just what we find. No doubt there is one point in which my analogy of the schoolboy breaks down. The English poetry which he reads when he ought to be doing Greek exercises may be just as good as the Greek poetry to which the exercises are leading him, so that in fixing on Milton instead of journeying on to Aeschylus his desire is not embracing a false object. But our case is very different. If a transtemporal, transfinite good is our real destiny, then any other good on which our desire fixes must be in some degree fallacious, must bear at best only a symbolical relation to what will truly satisfy.

In speaking of this desire for our own far-off country, which we find in ourselves even now, I feel a certain shyness. I am almost committing an indecency. I am trying to rip open the inconsolable secret in each one of you—the secret which hurts so much that you take your revenge on it by calling it names like Nostalgia and Romanticism and Adolescence; the secret also which pierces with such sweetness that when, in very intimate conversation, the mention of it becomes imminent, we grow awkward and affect to laugh at ourselves; the secret we cannot hide and cannot tell, though we desire to do both. We cannot tell it because it is a desire for something that has never actually appeared in our experience. We cannot hide it because our experience is constantly suggesting it, and we betray ourselves like lovers at the mention of a name. Our commonest expedient is to call it beauty and behave as if that had settled the matter. Wordsworth's expedient was to identify it with certain moments in his own past. But all this is a cheat. If Wordsworth had gone back to those moments in the past, he would not have found the thing itself, but only the reminder of it; what he remembered would turn out to be itself a remembering. The books or the music in which we thought the beauty was located will betray us if we trust to them; it was not *in* them, it only came *through* them, and what came through them was longing. These things—the beauty, the memory of our own past—are good images of what we really desire; but if they are mistaken for the thing itself, they turn into dumb idols, breaking the hearts of their worshippers. For they are not the thing itself; they are only the scent of a flower we have not found, the echo of a tune we have not heard, news from a country we have never yet visited. Do you think I am trying to weave a spell? Perhaps I am; but remember your fairy tales. Spells are used for breaking enchantments as well as for inducing them. And you and I have need of the strongest spell that can be found to wake us from the evil enchantment of worldliness which has been laid upon us for nearly a hundred years. Almost our whole education has been directed to silencing this shy, persistent, inner voice; almost all our modern philosophies have been devised to convince us that the good of man is to be found on this earth. And yet it is a remarkable thing that such philosophies of Progress or Creative Evolution themselves bear reluctant witness to the truth that our real goal is elsewhere. When they want to convince you that earth is your home, notice how they set about it. They begin by trying to persuade you that earth can be made into heaven, thus giving a sop to your sense of exile in earth as it is. Next, they tell you that this fortunate event is still a good way off in the future, thus giving a sop to your knowledge that the fatherland is not here and now. Finally, lest your longing for the transtemporal should awake and spoil the whole affair, they use any rhetoric that comes to hand to keep out of your mind the recollection that even if all the happiness they promised could come to man on earth, yet still each generation would lose it by death, including the last generation of all, and the whole story would be nothing, not even a story, for ever and ever. Hence all the nonsense that Mr. Shaw puts into the final speech of Lilith, and Bergson's remark that the *élan vital* is capable of surmounting all obstacles, perhaps even death—as if we could believe that any social or biological development on this planet will delay the senility of the sun or reverse the second law of thermodynamics.

Do what they will, then, we remain conscious of a desire which no natural happiness will satisfy. But is there any reason to suppose that reality offers any satisfaction to it? 'Nor does the being hungry prove that we have bread.' But I think it may be urged that this misses the point. A man's physical hunger does not prove that man will get any bread; he may die of starvation on a raft in the Atlantic. But surely a man's hunger does prove that he comes of a race which re-pairs its body by eating and inhabits a world where eatable substances exist. In the same way, though I do not believe (I wish I did) that my desire for Paradise proves that I shall enjoy it, I think it a pretty good indication that such a thing exists and that some men will. A man may love a woman and not win her; but it would be very odd if the phenomenon called 'falling in love' occurred in a sexless world.

Here, then, is the desire, still wandering and un-
certain of its object and still largely unable to see that
object in the direction where it really lies. Our sacred
books give us some account of the object. It is, of
course, a symbolical account. Heaven is, by definition,
outside our experience, but all intelligible descriptions
must be of things within our experience. The scriptural picture of heaven is therefore just as symbolical
as the picture which our desire, unaided, invents for
itself; heaven is not really full of jewellery any more
than it is really the beauty of Nature, or a fine piece
of music. The difference is that the scriptural imagery
has authority. It comes to us from writers who were
closer to God than we, and it has stood the test of
Christian experience down the centuries. The natural
appeal of this authoritative imagery is to me, at first,
very small. At first sight it chills, rather than awakes,
my desire. And that is just what I ought to expect. If
Christianity could tell me no more of the far-off land
than my own temperament led me to surmise already,
then Christianity would be no higher than myself. If

it has more to give me, I expect it to be less immediately attractive than 'my own stuff.' Sophocles at first seems dull and cold to the boy who has only reached Shelley. If our religion is something objective, then we must never avert our eyes from those elements in it which seem puzzling or repellent; for it will be precisely the puzzling or the repellent which conceals what we do not yet know and need to know.

The promises of Scripture may very roughly be reduced to five heads. It is promised (1) that we shall be with Christ; (2) that we shall be like Him; (3) with an enormous wealth of imagery, that we shall have 'glory'; (4) that we shall, in some sense, be fed or feasted or entertained; and (5) that we shall have some sort of official position in the universe—ruling cities, judging angels, being pillars of God's temple. The first question I ask about these promises is 'Why any one of them except the first?' Can anything be added to the conception of being with Christ? For it must be true, as an old writer says, that he who has God and everything else has no more than he who has God only. I think the answer turns again on the nature of symbols. For though it may escape our notice at first glance, yet it is true that any conception of being with Christ which most of us can now form will be not very much less symbolical than the other promises; for it will smuggle in ideas of proximity in space and loving conversation as we now understand conversation, and it will probably concentrate on the humanity of Christ to the exclusion of His deity. And, in fact, we find that those Christians who attend solely to this first promise always do fill it up with very earthly imagery indeed—in fact, with hymeneal or erotic imagery. I am not for a moment condemning such imagery. I heartily wish I could enter into it more deeply than I do, and pray that I yet shall. But my point is that this also is only a symbol, like the reality in some respects, but unlike it in others, and therefore needs correction from the different symbols in the other promises. The variation of the promises does not mean that anything other than God will be our ultimate bliss; but because God is more than a Person, and lest we should imagine the joy of His presence too exclusively in terms of our present poor experience of personal love, with all its narrowness and strain and monotony, a dozen changing images, correcting and relieving each other, are supplied.

I turn next to the idea of glory. There is no getting away from the fact that this idea is very prominent in the New Testament and in early Christian writings. Salvation is constantly associated with palms, crowns, white robes, thrones, and splendour like the sun and stars. All this makes no immediate appeal to me at all, and in that respect I fancy I am a typical modern. Glory suggests two ideas to me, of which one seems wicked and the other ridiculous. Either glory means to me fame, or it means luminosity. As for the first, since to be famous means to be better known than other people, the desire for fame appears to me as a competitive passion and therefore of hell rather than heaven. As for the second, who wishes to become a kind of living electric light bulb?

When I began to look into this matter I was shocked to find such different Christians as Milton, Johnson, and Thomas Aquinas taking heavenly glory quite frankly in the sense of fame or good report. But not fame conferred by our fellow creatures—fame with God, approval or (I might say) 'appreciation' by God. And then, when I had thought it over, I saw that this view was scriptural; nothing can eliminate from the parable the divine *accolade*, 'Well done, thou good and faithful servant.' With that, a good deal of what I had been thinking all my life fell down like a house of cards. I suddenly remembered that no one can enter heaven except as a child; and nothing is so obvious in a child—not in a conceited child, but in a good child—as its great and undisguised pleasure in being praised. Not only in a child, either, but even in a dog or a horse. Apparently what I had mistaken for humility had, all these years, prevented me from understanding what is in fact the humblest, the most childlike, the most creaturely of pleasures—nay, the specific pleasure of the inferior: the pleasure of a beast before men, a child before its father, a pupil before his teacher, a creature before its Creator. I am not forgetting how horribly this most innocent desire is parodied in our human ambitions, or how very quickly, in my own experience, the lawful pleasure of praise from those whom it was my duty to please turns into the deadly poison of self-admiration. But I thought I could detect a moment—a very, very short moment—before this happened, during which the satisfaction of having pleased those whom I rightly loved and rightly feared was pure. And that is enough to raise our thoughts to what may happen when the redeemed soul, beyond all hope and nearly beyond belief, learns at last that she has pleased Him whom she was created to please. There will be no room for vanity then. She will be free from the miserable illusion that it is her doing. With no taint of what we should now call self-approval she will most innocently rejoice in the thing that God has made her to be, and the moment which heals her old inferiority complex forever will also drown her pride deeper than Prospero's book. Perfect humility dispenses with modesty. If God is satisfied with the work, the work may be satisfied with itself; 'it is not for her to bandy compliments with her Sovereign.' I can imagine someone saying that he dislikes my idea of heaven as a place where we are patted on the back. But proud misunderstanding is behind that dislike. In the end that Face which is the delight or the terror of the universe must be turned upon each of us either with one expression or with the other, either conferring glory inexpressible or inflicting shame that can never be cured or disguised. I read in a periodical the other day that the fundamental thing is how we think of God. By God Himself, it is not! How God thinks of us is not only more important, but infinitely more important. Indeed, how we think of Him is of no importance except insofar as it is related to how He thinks of us. It is written that we shall 'stand before' Him, shall appear, shall be inspected. The promise of glory is the promise, almost incredible and only possible by the work of Christ, that some of us, that any of us who really chooses, shall actually survive that examination, shall find approval, shall please God. To please God . . . to be a real ingredient in the divine happiness . . . to be loved by God, not merely pitied, but delighted in as an artist delights in his work or a father in a son—it seems impossible, a weight or burden of glory which our thoughts can hardly sustain. But so it is.

And now notice what is happening. If I had rejected the authoritative and scriptural image of glory and stuck obstinately to the vague desire which was, at the outset, my only pointer to heaven, I could have seen no connection at all between that desire and the Christian promise. But now, having followed up what seemed puzzling and repellent in the sacred books, I find, to my great surprise, looking back, that the connection is perfectly clear. Glory, as Christianity teaches me to hope for it, turns out to satisfy my original desire and indeed to reveal an element in that desire which I had not noticed. By ceasing for a moment to consider my own wants I have begun to learn better what I really wanted. When I attempted, a few minutes ago, to describe our spiritual longings,

I was omitting one of their most curious characteristics. We usually notice it just as the moment of vision dies away, as the music ends, or as the landscape loses the celestial light. What we feel then has been well described by Keats as 'the journey homeward to habitual self.' You know what I mean. For a few minutes we have had the illusion of belonging to that world. Now we wake to find that it is no such thing. We have been mere spectators. Beauty has smiled, but not to welcome us; her face was turned in our direction, but not to see us. We have not been accepted, welcomed, or taken into the dance. We may go when we please, we may stay if we can: 'Nobody marks us.' A scientist may reply that since most of the things we call beautiful are inanimate, it is not very surprising that they take no notice of us. That, of course, is true. It is not the physical objects that I am speaking of, but that indescribable something of which they become for a moment the messengers. And part of the bitterness which mixes with the sweetness of that message is due to the fact that it so seldom seems to be a message intended for us, but rather something we have overheard. By bitterness I mean pain, not resentment. We should hardly dare to ask that any notice be taken of ourselves. But we pine. The sense that in this universe we are treated as strangers, the longing to be acknowledged, to meet with some response, to bridge some chasm that yawns between us and reality, is part of our inconsolable secret. And surely, from this point of view, the promise of glory, in the sense described, becomes highly relevant to our deep desire. For glory means good rapport with God, acceptance by God, response, acknowledgement, and welcome into the heart of things. The door on which we have been knocking all our lives will open at last.

Perhaps it seems rather crude to describe glory as the fact of being 'noticed' by God. But this is almost the language of the New Testament. St. Paul promises to those who love God not, as we should expect, that they will know Him, but that they will be known by Him (1 Cor. 8:3). It is a strange promise. Does not God know all things at all times? But it is dreadfully reechoed in another passage of the New Testament. There we are warned that it may happen to anyone of us to appear at last before the face of God and hear only the appalling words, 'I never knew you. Depart from Me.' In some sense, as dark to the intellect as it is unendurable to the feelings, we can be both banished from the presence of Him who is present everywhere and erased from the knowledge of Him who knows all. We can be left utterly and absolutely *outside*— repelled, exiled, estranged, finally and unspeakably ignored. On the other hand, we can be called in, welcomed, received, acknowledged. We walk every day on the razor edge between these two incredible possibilities. Apparently, then, our lifelong nostalgia, our longing to be reunited with something in the universe from which we now feel cut off, to be on the inside of some door which we have always seen from the outside, is no mere neurotic fancy, but the truest index of our real situation. And to be at last summoned inside would be both glory and honour beyond all our merits and also the healing of that old ache.

And this brings me to the other sense of glory—glory as brightness, splendour, luminosity. We are to shine as the sun, we are to be given the Morning Star. I think I begin to see what it means. In one way, of course, God has given us the Morning Star already: you can go and enjoy the gift on many fine mornings if you get up early enough. What more, you may ask, do we want? Ah, but we want so much more—something the books on aesthetics take little notice of. But the poets and the mythologies know all about it. We do not want merely to *see* beauty, though, God knows, even that is bounty enough. We want something else which can hardly be put into words—to be united with the beauty we see, to pass into it, to receive it into ourselves, to bathe in it, to become part of it. That is why we have peopled air and earth and water with gods and goddesses and nymphs and elves—that, though we cannot, yet these projections can enjoy in themselves that beauty, grace, and power of which Nature is the image. That is why the poets tell us such lovely falsehoods. They talk as if the west wind could really sweep into a human soul; but it can't. They tell us that 'beauty born of murmuring sound' will pass into a human face; but it won't. Or not yet. For if we take the imagery of Scripture seriously, if we believe that God will one day *give* us the Morning Star and cause us to *put on* the splendour of the sun, then we may surmise that both the ancient myths and the modern poetry, so false as history, may be very near the truth as prophecy. At present we are on the outside of the world, the wrong side of the door. We discern the freshness and purity of morning, but they do not make us fresh and pure. We cannot mingle with the splendours we see. But all the leaves of the New Testament are rustling with the rumour that it will not always be so. Some day, God willing, we shall get *in*. When human souls have become as perfect in voluntary obedience as the inanimate creation is in its lifeless obedience, then they will put on its glory, or rather that greater glory of which Nature is only the first sketch. For you must not think that I am putting forward any heathen fancy of being absorbed into Nature. Nature is mortal; we shall outlive her. When all the suns and nebulae have passed away, each one of you will still be alive. Nature is only the image, the symbol; but it is the symbol Scripture invites me to use. We are summoned to pass in through Nature, beyond her, into that splendour which she fitfully reflects.

And in there, in beyond Nature, we shall eat of the tree of life. At present, if we are reborn in Christ, the spirit in us lives directly on God; but the mind and, still more, the body receives life from Him at a thousand removes—through our ancestors, through our food, through the elements. The faint, far-off results of those energies which God's creative rapture implanted in matter when He made the worlds are what we now call physical pleasures; and even thus filtered, they are too much for our present management. What would it be to taste at the fountainhead that stream of which even these lower reaches prove so intoxicating? Yet that, I believe, is what lies before us. The whole man is to drink joy from the fountain of joy. As St. Augustine said, the rapture of the saved soul will 'flow over' into the glorified body. In the light of our present specialised and depraved appetites, we cannot imagine this *torrens voluptatis*, and I warn everyone most seriously not to try. But it must be mentioned, to drive out thoughts even more misleading—thoughts that what is saved is a mere ghost, or that the risen body lives in numb insensibility. The body was made for the Lord, and these dismal fancies are wide of the mark.

Meanwhile the cross comes before the crown and tomorrow is a Monday morning. A cleft has opened in the pitiless walls of the world, and we are invited to follow our great Captain inside. The following Him is, of course, the essential point. That being so, it may be asked what practical use there is in the speculations which I have been indulging. I can think of at least one such use. It may be possible for each to think too much of his own potential glory hereafter; it is hardly possible for him to think too often or too deeply about that of his neighbour. The load, or weight, or burden of my neighbour's glory should be laid on my back, a load so heavy that only humility can carry it, and the backs of the proud will be broken. It is a serious thing to live in a society of possible gods and goddesses, to remember that the dullest and most uninteresting person you can talk to may one day be a creature which, if you saw it now, you would be strongly tempted to worship, or else a horror and a corruption such as you now meet, if at all, only in a nightmare. All day long we are, in some degree, helping each other to one or other of these destinations. It is in the light of these overwhelming possibilities, it is with the awe and the circumspection proper to them, that we should conduct all our dealings with one another, all friendships, all loves, all play, all politics. There are no *ordinary* people. You have never talked to a mere mortal. Nations, cultures, arts, civilisations—these are mortal, and their life is to ours as the life of a gnat. But it is immortals whom we joke with, work with, marry, snub, and exploit—immortal horrors or everlasting splendours. This does not mean that we are to be perpetually solemn. We must play. But our merriment must be of that kind (and it is, in fact, the merriest kind) which exists between people who have, from the outset, taken each other seriously—no flippancy, no superiority, no presumption. And our charity must be a real and costly love, with deep feeling for the sins in spite of which we love the sinner—no mere tolerance, or indulgence which parodies love as flippancy parodies merriment. Next to the Blessed Sacrament itself, your neighbour is the holiest object presented to your senses. If he is your Christian neighbour, he is holy in almost the same way, for in him also Christ *vere latitat*—the glorifier and the glorified, Glory Himself, is truly hidden.

ON NOT FEELING THREATENED WHEN CHRISTIANITY REMAINS UNCHANGED WHILE SCIENCE AND KNOWLEDGE PROGRESSES

WHEREVER THERE IS real progress in knowledge, there is some knowledge that is not superseded. Indeed, the very possibility of progress demands that there should be an unchanging element. New bottles for new wine, by all means: but not new palates, throats, and stomachs, or it would not be, for us, 'wine' at all. I take it we should all agree to find this sort of

God in the Dock, from the chapter titled
"Dogma and the Universe."

unchanging element in the simple rules of mathematics. I would add to these the primary principles of morality. And I would also add the fundamental doctrines of Christianity. To put it in rather more technical language, I claim that the positive historical statements made by Christianity have the power, elsewhere found chiefly in formal principles, of receiving, without intrinsic change, the increasing complexity of meaning which increasing knowledge puts into them.

For example, it may be true (though I don't for a moment suppose it is) that when the Nicene Creed said 'He came down from Heaven', the writers had in mind a local movement from a local heaven to the surface of the earth—like a parachute descent. Others since may have dismissed the idea of a spatial heaven altogether. But neither the significance nor the credibility of what is asserted seems to be in the least affected by the change. On either view, the thing is miraculous: on either view, the mental images which attend the act of belief are inessential. When an uneducated convert and a Harley Street specialist both affirm that Christ rose from the dead, there is, no doubt, a very great difference between their thoughts. To one, the simple picture of a dead body getting up is sufficient; the other may think of a whole series of biochemical and even physical processes beginning to work backwards. The doctor knows that, in his experience, they never have worked backwards; but the uneducated convert knows that dead bodies don't get up and walk. Both are faced with miracle, and both know it. If both think miracle impossible, the only difference is that the doctor will expound the impossibility in much greater detail, will give an elaborate gloss on the simple statement that dead men don't walk about. If both believe, all the doctor says will merely analyze and explicate the words 'He rose.' When the author of Genesis says that God made man in His own image, he may have pictured a vaguely corporeal God making man as a child makes a figure out of plasticine. A modern Christian philosopher may think of a process lasting from the first creation of matter to the final appearance on this planet of an organism fit to receive spiritual as well as biological life. But both mean essentially the same thing. Both are denying the same thing—the doctrine that matter by some blind power inherent in itself has produced spirituality.

Does this mean that Christians on different levels of general education conceal radically different beliefs under an identical form of words? Certainly not. For what they agree on is the substance, and what they differ about is the shadow. When one imagines his God seated in a local heaven above a flat earth, where another sees God and creation in terms of Professor Whitehead's philosophy,[1] this difference touches precisely what does not matter. Perhaps this seems to you an exaggeration. But is it? As regards material reality, we are now being forced to the conclusion that we know nothing about it save its mathematics. The tangible beach and pebbles of our first calculators, the imaginable atoms of Democritus, the plain man's picture of space, turn out to be the shadow; numbers are the substance of our knowledge, the sole liaison between mind and things. What nature is in herself evades us; what seem to naive perception to be the evident things about her, turn out to be the most phantasmal. It is something the same with our knowledge of spiritual reality. What God is in Himself, how He is to be conceived by philosophers, retreats continually from our knowledge. The elaborate world-pictures which accompany religion and which look each so solid while they last, turn out to be only shadows. It is religion itself—prayer and sacrament and repentance and adoration—which is here, in the long run, our sole avenue to the real. Like mathematics, religion can grow from within, or decay. The Jew knows more than the Pagan, the Christian more than the Jew, the modern vaguely religious man less than any of the three. But, like mathematics, it remains simply itself, capable of being applied to any new theory of the material universe and outmoded by none.

When any man comes into the presence of God he will find, whether he wishes it or not, that all those things which seemed to make him so different from the men of other times, or even from his earlier self, have fallen off him. He is back where he always was, where every man always is. *Eadem sunt omnia semper*[2]. Do not let us deceive ourselves. No possible complexity which we can give to our picture of the universe can hide us from God: there is no copse, no forest, no jungle thick enough to provide cover. We read in Revelation of Him that sat on the throne 'from whose face the earth and heaven fled away.'[3] It may happen to any of us at any moment. In the twinkling of an eye, in a time too small to be measured, and in any place, all that seems to divide us from God can flee away, vanish, leaving us naked before Him, like the first man, like the only man, as if nothing but He and I existed. And since that contact cannot be avoided for long, and since it means either bliss or horror, the business of life is to learn to like it. That is the first and great commandment.

---

[1] Alfred North Whitehead (1861–1947), who wrote, among other works, *Science and the Modern World* (1925) and *Religion in the Making* (1926).

[2] 'Everything is always the same.'

[3] Revelation 20:11.

ON THE IMPORTANCE OF
PRACTICING CHARITY

AS TO THE meaning of the word, 'Charity' now means simply what used to be called 'alms'—that is, giving to the poor. Originally it had a much wider meaning. (You can see how it got the modern sense. If a man has 'charity, giving to the poor is one of the most obvious things he does, and so people came to talk as if that were the whole of charity. In the same way, 'rhyme' is the most obvious thing about poetry, and so people come to mean by 'poetry' simply rhyme and nothing more.) Charity means 'Love, in the Christian sense.' But love, in the Christian sense,

---

Mere Christianity, from the chapter titled "Charity."

does not mean an emotion. It is a state not of the feelings but of the will; that state of the will which we have naturally about ourselves, and must learn to have about other people.

I pointed out in the chapter on Forgiveness that our love for ourselves does not mean that we *like* ourselves. It means that we wish our own good. In the same way Christian Love (or Charity) for our neighbours is quite a different thing from liking or affection. We 'like' or are 'fond of' some people, and not of others. It is important to understand that this natural 'liking' is neither a sin nor a virtue, any more than your likes and dislikes in food are a sin or a virtue. It is just a fact. But, of course, what we do about it is either sinful or virtuous.

Natural liking or affection for people makes it easier to be 'charitable' towards them. It is, therefore, normally a duty to encourage our affections—to 'like' people as much as we can (just as it is often our duty to encourage our liking for exercise or wholesome food)—not because this liking is itself the virtue of charity, but because it is a help to it. On the other hand, it is also necessary to keep a very sharp look-out for fear our liking for some one person makes us uncharitable, or even unfair, to someone else. There are even cases where our liking conflicts with our charity towards the person we like. For example, a doting mother may be tempted by natural affection to 'spoil' her child; that is, to gratify her own affectionate impulses at the expense of the child's real happiness later on.

But though natural likings should normally be encouraged, it would be quite wrong to think that the way to become charitable is to sit trying to manufacture affectionate feelings. Some people are 'cold' by temperament; that may be a misfortune for them, but it is no more a sin than having a bad digestion is a sin; and it does not cut them out from the chance, or excuse them from the duty, of learning charity. The rule for all of us is perfectly simple. Do not waste time bothering whether you 'love' your neighbour; act as if you did. As soon as we do this we find one of the great secrets. When you are behaving as if you loved someone, you will presently come to love him. If you injure someone you dislike, you will find yourself disliking him more. If you do him a good turn, you will find yourself disliking him less. There is, indeed, one exception. If you do him a good turn, not to please God and obey the law of charity, but to show him what a fine forgiving chap you are, and to put him in your debt, and then sit down to wait for his 'gratitude', you will probably be disappointed. (People are not fools: they have a very quick eye for anything like showing off, or patronage.) But whenever we do good to another self, just because it is a self, made (like us) by God, and desiring its own happiness as we desire ours, we shall have learned to love it a little more or, at least, to dislike it less.

Consequently, though Christian charity sounds a very cold thing to people whose heads are full of sentimentality, and though it is quite distinct from affection, yet it leads to affection. The difference between a Christian and a worldly man is not that the worldly man has only affections or 'likings' and the Christian has only 'charity.' The worldly man treats certain people kindly because he 'likes' them: the Christian, trying to treat every one kindly, finds himself liking more and more people as he goes on—including people he could not even have imagined himself liking at the beginning.

This same spiritual law works terribly in the opposite direction. The Germans, perhaps, at first ill-treated the Jews because they hated them: afterwards they hated them much more because they had ill-treated them. The more cruel you are, the more you will hate; and the more you hate, the more cruel you will become—and so on in a vicious circle for ever.

Good and evil both increase at compound interest. That is why the little decisions you and I make every day are of such infinite importance. The smallest good act today is the capture of a strategic point from which, a few months later, you may be able to go on to victories you never dreamed of. An apparently trivial indulgence in lust or anger today is the loss of a ridge or railway line or bridgehead from which the enemy may launch an attack otherwise impossible.

Some writers use the word charity to describe not only Christian love between human beings, but also God's love for man and man's love for God. About the second of these two, people are often worried. They are told they ought to love God. They cannot find any such feeling in themselves. What are they to do? The answer is the same as before. Act as if you did. Do not sit trying to manufacture feelings. Ask yourself, 'If I were sure that I loved God, what would I do?' When you have found the answer, go and do it.

On the whole, God's love for us is a much safer subject to think about than our love for Him. Nobody can always have devout feelings: and even if we could, feelings are not what God principally cares about. Christian Love, either towards God or towards man, is an affair of the will. If we are trying to do His will we are obeying the commandment, 'Thou shalt love the Lord thy God.' He will give us feelings of love if He pleases. We cannot create them for ourselves, and we must not demand them as a right. But the great thing to remember is that, though our feelings come and go, His love for us does not. It is not wearied by our sins, or our indifference; and, therefore, it is quite relentless in its determination that we shall be cured of those sins, at whatever cost to us, at whatever cost to Him.

ON WHAT IT MEANS
TO BE PART OF THE
BODY OF CHRIST

NO CHRISTIAN AND, indeed, no historian could accept the epigram which defines religion as 'what a man does with his solitude.' It was one of the Wesleys, I think, who said that the New Testament knows nothing of solitary religion. We are forbidden to neglect the assembling of ourselves together. Christianity is already institutional in the earliest of its documents. The Church is the Bride of Christ. We are members of one another.

In our own age the idea that religion belongs to

The Weight of Glory, from the chapter titled "Membership."

our private life—that it is, in fact, an occupation for the individual's hour of leisure—is at once paradoxical, dangerous, and natural. It is paradoxical because this exaltation of the individual in the religious field springs up in an age when collectivism is ruthlessly defeating the individual in every other field. I see this even in a university. When I first went to Oxford the typical undergraduate society consisted of a dozen men, who knew one another intimately, hearing a paper by one of their own number in a small sitting-room and hammering out their problem till one or two in the morning. Before the war the typical undergraduate society had come to be a mixed audience of one or two hundred students assembled in a public hall to hear a lecture from some visiting celebrity. Even on those rare occasions when a modern undergraduate is not attending some such society he is seldom engaged in those solitary walks, or walks with a single companion, which built the minds of the previous generations. He lives in a crowd; caucus has replaced friendship. And this tendency not only exists both within and without the university, but is often approved. There is a crowd of busy-bodies, self-appointed masters of ceremonies, whose life is devoted to destroying solitude wherever solitude still exists. They call it 'taking the young people out of themselves', or 'waking them up', or 'overcoming their apathy'. If an Augustine, a Vaughan, a Traherne, or a Wordsworth should be born in the modern world, the leaders of a youth organization would soon cure him. If a really good home, such as the home of Alcinous and Arete in the *Odyssey* or the Rostovs in *War and Peace* or any of Charlotte M. Yonge's families, existed today, it would be denounced as *bourgeois* and every engine of destruction would be levelled against it. And even where the planners fail and someone is left physically by himself, the wireless has seen to it that he will be—in a sense not intended by Scipio—never less alone than when alone. We live, in fact, in a world starved for solitude, silence, and privacy, and therefore starved for meditation and true friendship.

That religion should be relegated to solitude in such an age is, then, paradoxical. But it is also dangerous for two reasons. In the first place, when the modern world says to us aloud, 'You may be religious when you are alone,' it adds under its breath, 'and I will see to it that you never are alone.' To make Christianity a private affair while banishing all privacy is to relegate it to the rainbow's end or the Greek calends. That is one of the enemy's stratagems. In the second place, there is the danger that real Christians who know that Christianity is not a solitary affair may react against that error by simply transporting into our spiritual life that same collectivism which has already conquered our secular life. That is the enemy's other stratagem. Like a good chess player, he is always trying to manoeuvre you into a position where you can save your castle only by losing your bishop. In order to avoid the trap we must insist that though the private conception of Christianity is an error, it is a profoundly natural one and is clumsily attempting to guard a great truth. Behind it is the obvious feeling that our modern collectivism is an outrage upon human nature and that from this, as from all other evils, God will be our shield and buckler.

This feeling is just. As personal and private life is lower than participation in the Body of Christ, so the collective life is lower than the personal and private life and has no value save in its service. The secular community, since it exists for our natural good and not for our supernatural, has no higher end than to facilitate and safeguard the family, and friendship, and solitude. To be happy at home, said Johnson, is the end of all human endeavour. As long as we are thinking only of natural values we must say that the sun looks down on nothing half so good as a household laughing together over a meal, or two friends talking over a pint of beer, or a man alone reading a book that interests him; and that all economies, politics, laws, armies, and institutions, save insofar as they prolong and multiply such scenes, are a mere ploughing the sand and sowing the ocean, a meaningless vanity and vexation of spirit. Collective activities are, of course, necessary, but this is the end to which they are necessary. Great sacrifices of this private happiness by those who have it may be necessary in order that it may be more widely distributed. All may have to be a little hungry in order that none may starve. But do not let us mistake necessary evils for good. The mistake is easily made. Fruit has to be tinned if it is to be transported and has to lose thereby some of its good qualities. But one meets people who have learned actually to prefer the tinned fruit to the fresh. A sick society must think much about politics, as a sick man must think much about his digestion; to ignore the subject may be fatal cowardice for the one as for the other. But if either comes to regard it as the natural food of the mind—if either forgets that we think of such things only in order to be able to think of something else—then what was undertaken for the sake of health has become itself a new and deadly disease.

There is, in fact, a fatal tendency in all human activities for the means to encroach upon the very ends which they were intended to serve. Thus money comes to hinder the exchange of commodities, and rules of art to hamper genius, and examinations to prevent young men from becoming learned. It does not, unfortunately, always follow that the encroaching means can be dispensed with. I think it probable that the collectivism of our life is necessary and will increase, and I think that our only safeguard against its deathly properties is in a Christian life, for we were promised that we could handle serpents and drink deadly things and yet live. That is the truth behind the erroneous definition of religion with which we started. Where it went wrong was in opposing to the collective mass, mere solitude. But that is of course a mere matter of opinion. The Christian is called not to individualism but to membership in the mystical body. A consideration of the differences between the secular collective and the mystical body is therefore the first step to understanding how Christianity without being individualistic can yet counteract collectivism.

At the outset we are hampered by a difficulty of language. The very word *membership* is of Christian origin, but it has been taken over by the world and emptied of all meaning. In any book on logic you may see the expression 'members of a class'. It must be most emphatically stated that the items or particulars included in a homogeneous class are almost the reverse of what St. Paul meant by *members*. By *members* ([Greek]) he meant what we should call *organs*, things essentially different from, and complementary to, one another, things differing not only in structure and function but also in dignity. Thus, in a club, the committee as a whole and the servants as a whole may both properly be regarded as 'members'; what we should call the members of the club are merely units. A row of identically dressed and identically trained soldiers set side by side, or a number of citizens listed as voters in a constituency are not members of anything in the Pauline sense. I am afraid that when we describe a man as 'a member of the Church' we usually mean nothing Pauline; we mean only that he is a unit—that he is one more specimen of some kind of things as X and Y and Z. How true membership in a body differs from inclusion in a collective may be seen in the structure of a family. The grandfather, the parents, the grown-up son, the child, the dog, and the cat are true members (in the organic sense), precisely because they are not members or units of a homogeneous class. They are not interchangeable. Each person is almost a species in himself. The mother is not simply a different person from the daughter; she is a different kind of person. The grownup brother is not simply one unit in the class children; he is a separate estate of the realm. The father and grandfather are almost as different as the cat and the dog. If you subtract any one member, you have not simply reduced the family in number; you have inflicted an injury on its structure. Its unity is a unity of unlikes, almost of incommensurables.

A dim perception of the richness inherent in this kind of unity is one reason why we enjoy a book like *The Wind in the Willows;* a trio such as Rat, Mole, and Badger symbolises the extreme differentiation of persons in harmonious union, which we know intuitively to be our true refuge both from solitude and from the collective. The affection between such oddly matched couples as Dick Swiveller and the Marchioness, or Mr. Pickwick and Sam Weller pleases in the same way. That is why the modern notion that children should call their parents by their Christian names is so perverse. For this is an effort to ignore the difference in kind which makes for real organic unity. They are trying to inoculate the child with the preposterous view that one's mother is simply a fellow citizen like anyone else, to make it ignorant of what all men know and insensible to what all men feel. They are trying to drag the featureless repetitions of the collective into the fuller and more concrete world of the family.

A convict has a number instead of a name. That is the collective idea carried to its extreme. But a man in his own house may also lose his name, because he is called simply 'Father'. That is membership in a body. The loss of the name in both cases reminds us that there are two opposite ways of departing from isolation.

The society into which the Christian is called at baptism is not a collective but a Body. It is in fact that Body of which the family is an image on the natural level. If anyone came to it with the misconception that membership of the Church was membership in a debased modern sense—a massing together of persons as if they were pennies or counters—he would be corrected at the threshold by the discovery that the head of this Body is so unlike the inferior members that they share no predicate with Him save by analogy. We are summoned from the outset to combine as creatures with our Creator, as mortals with immortal, as redeemed sinners with sinless Redeemer. His presence, the interaction between Him and us, must always be the overwhelmingly dominant factor in the life we are to lead within the Body, and any conception of Christian fellowship which does not mean primarily fellowship with Him is out of court. After that it seems almost trivial to trace further down the diversity of operations to the unity of the Spirit. But it is very plainly there. There are priests divided from the laity, catechumens divided from those who are in full fellowship. There is authority of husbands over wives and parents over children. There is, in forms too subtle for official embodiment, a continual interchange of complementary ministrations. We are all constantly teaching and learning, forgiving and being forgiven, representing Christ to man when we intercede, and man to Christ when others intercede for us. The sacrifice of selfish privacy which is daily demanded of us is daily repaid a hundredfold in the true growth of personality which the life of the Body encourages. Those who are members of one another become as diverse as the hand and the ear. That is why the worldlings are so monotonously alike compared with the almost fantastic variety of the saints. Obedience is the road to freedom, humility the road to pleasure, unity the road to personality.

And now I must say something that may appear to you a paradox. You have often heard that though in the world we hold different stations, yet we are all equal in the sight of God. There are, of course, senses in which this is true. God is no accepter of persons; His love for us is not measured by our social rank or our intellectual talents. But I believe there is a sense in which this maxim is the reverse of the truth. I am going to venture to say that artificial equality is necessary in the life of the State, but that in the Church we strip off this disguise, we recover our real inequalities, and are thereby refreshed and quickened.

I believe in political equality. But there are two opposite reasons for being a democrat. You may think all men so good that they deserve a share in the government of the commonwealth, and so wise that the commonwealth needs their advice. That is, in my opinion, the false, romantic doctrine of democracy. On the other hand, you may believe fallen men to be so wicked that not one of them can be trusted with any irresponsible power over his fellows.

That I believe to be the true ground of democracy. I do not believe that God created an egalitarian world. I believe the authority of parent over child, husband over wife, learned over simple to have been as much a part of the original plan as the authority of man over beast. I believe that if we had not fallen, Filmer would be right, and patriarchal monarchy would be the sole lawful government. But since we have learned sin, we have found, as Lord Acton says, that 'all power corrupts, and absolute power corrupts absolutely'. The only remedy has been to take away the powers and substitute a legal fiction of equality. The authority of father and husband has been rightly abolished on the legal plane, not because this authority is in itself bad (on the contrary, it is, I hold, divine in origin), but because fathers and husbands are bad. Theocracy has been rightly abolished not because it is bad that learned priests should govern ignorant laymen, but because priests are wicked men like the rest of us. Even the authority of man over beast has had to be interfered with because it is constantly abused.

Equality is for me in the same position as clothes. It is a result of the Fall and the remedy for it. Any attempt to retrace the steps by which we have arrived at egalitarianism and to reintroduce the old authorities on the political level is for me as foolish as it would be to take off our clothes. The Nazi and the nudist make the same mistake. But it is the naked body, still there beneath the clothes of each one of us, which really lives. It is the hierarchical world, still alive and (very properly) hidden behind a façade of equal citizenship, which is our real concern.

Do not misunderstand me. I am not in the least belittling the value of this egalitarian fiction which is our only defence against one another's cruelty. I should view with the strongest disapproval any proposal to abolish manhood suffrage, or the Married Women's Property Act. But the function of equality is purely protective. It is medicine, not food. By treating human persons (in judicious defiance of the observed facts) as if they were all the same kind of thing, we avoid innumerable evils. But it is not on this that we were made to live. It is idle to say that men are of equal value. If value is taken in a worldly sense—if we mean that all men are equally useful or beautiful or good or entertaining—then it is nonsense. If it means that all are of equal value as immortal souls, then I think it conceals a dangerous error. The infinite value of each human soul is not a Christian doctrine. God did not die for man because of some value He perceived in him. The value of each human soul considered simply in itself, out of relation to God, is zero. As St. Paul writes, to have died for valuable men would have been not divine but merely heroic; but God died for sinners. He loved us not because we were lovable, but because He is Love. It may be that He loves all equally—He certainly loved all to the death—and I am not certain what the expression means. If there is equality, it is in His love, not in us.

Equality is a quantitative term and therefore love often knows nothing of it. Authority exercised with humility and obedience accepted with delight are the very lines along which our spirits live. Even in the life of the affections, much more in the Body of Christ, we step outside that world which says 'I am as good as you.' It is like turning from a march to a dance. It is like taking off our clothes. We become, as Chesterton said, taller when we bow; we become lowlier when we instruct. It delights me that there should be moments in the services of my own Church when the priest stands and I kneel. As democracy becomes more complete in the outer world and opportunities for reverence are successively removed, the refreshment, the cleansing, and invigorating returns to inequality, which the Church offers us, become more and more necessary.

In this way then, the Christian life defends the single personality from the collective, not by isolating him but by giving him the status of an organ in the mystical Body. As the Book of Revelation says, he is made 'a pillar in the temple of God'; and it adds, 'he shall go no more out'. That introduces a new side of our subject. That structural position in the Church which the humblest Christian occupies is eternal and even cosmic. The Church will outlive the universe; in it the individual person will outlive the universe. Everything that is joined to the immortal head will share His immortality. We hear little of this from the

Christian pulpit today. What has come of our silence may be judged from the fact that recently addressing the Forces on this subject, I found that one of my audience regarded this doctrine as 'theosophical'. If we do not believe it, let us be honest and relegate the Christian faith to museums. If we do, let us give up the pretence that it makes no difference. For this is the real answer to every excessive claim made by the collective. It is mortal; we shall live forever. There will come a time when every culture, every institution, every nation, the human race, all biological life is extinct and every one of us is still alive. Immortality is promised to us, not to these generalities. It was not for societies or states that Christ died, but for men. In that sense Christianity must seem to secular collectivists to involve an almost frantic assertion of individuality. But then it is not the individual as such who will share Christ's victory over death. We shall share the victory by being in the Victor. A rejection, or in Scripture's strong language, a crucifixion of the natural self is the passport to everlasting life. Nothing that has not died will be resurrected. That is just how Christianity cuts across the antithesis between individualism and collectivism. There lies the maddening ambiguity of our faith as it must appear to outsiders. It sets its face relentlessly against our natural individualism; on the other hand, it gives back to those who abandon individualism an eternal possession of their own personal being, even of their bodies. As mere biological entities, each with its separate will to live and to expand, we are apparently of no account; we are cross-fodder. But as organs in the Body of Christ, as stones and pillars in the temple, we are assured of our eternal self-identity and shall live to remember the galaxies as an old tale.

This may be put in another way. Personality is eternal and inviolable. But then, personality is not a datum from which we start. The individualism in which we all begin is only a parody or shadow of it. True personality lies ahead—how far ahead, for most of us, I dare not say. And the key to it does not lie in ourselves. It will not be attained by development from within outwards. It will come to us when we occupy those places in the structure of the eternal cosmos for which we were designed or invented. As a colour first reveals its true quality when placed by an excellent artist in its pre-elected spot between certain others, as a spice reveals its true flavour when inserted just where and when a good cook wishes among the other ingredients, as the dog becomes really doggy only when he has taken his place in the household of man, so we shall then first be true persons when we have suffered ourselves to be fitted into our places. We are marble waiting to be shaped, metal waiting to be run into a mould.

No doubt there are already, even in the unregenerate self, faint hints of what mould each is designed for, or what sort of pillar he will be. But it is, I think, a gross exaggeration to picture the saving of a soul as being, normally, at all like the development from seed to flower. The very words *repentance, regeneration, the New Man,* suggest something very different. Some tendencies in each natural man may have to be simply rejected. Our Lord speaks of eyes being plucked out and hands lopped off—a frankly Procrustean method of adaptation.

The reason we recoil from this is that we have in our day started by getting the whole picture upside down. Starting with the doctrine that every individuality is 'of infinite value', we then picture God as a kind of employment committee whose business it is to find suitable careers for souls, square holes for square pegs. In fact, however, the value of the individual does not lie in him. He is capable of receiving value. He receives it by union with Christ. There is no question of finding for him a place in the living temple which will do justice to his inherent value and give scope to his natural idiosyncrasy. The place was there first. The man was created for it. He will not be himself till he is there. We shall be true and everlasting and really divine persons only in Heaven, just as we are, even now, coloured bodies only in the light.

To say this is to repeat what everyone here admits already—that we are saved by grace, that in our flesh dwells no good thing, that we are, through and through, creatures not creators, derived beings, living not of ourselves but from Christ. If I seem to have complicated a simple matter, you will, I hope, forgive me. I have been anxious to bring out two points. I have wanted to try to expel that quite un-Christian worship of the human individual simply as such which is so rampant in modern thought side by side with our collectivism, for one error begets the opposite error and, far from neutralising, they aggravate each other. I mean the pestilent notion (one sees it in literary criticism) that each of us starts with a treasure called 'personality' locked up inside him, and that to expand and express this, to guard it from interference, to be 'original', is the main end of life. This is Pelagian, or worse, and it defeats even itself. No man who values originality will ever be original. But try to tell the truth as you see it, try to do any bit of work as well as it can be done for the work's sake, and what men call originality will come unsought. Even on that level, the submission of the individual to the function is already beginning to bring true personality to birth. And secondly, I have wanted to show that Christianity is not, in the long run, concerned either with individuals or communities. Neither the individual nor the community as popular thought understands them can inherit eternal life, neither the natural self, nor the collective mass, but a new creature.

ON PRACTICAL MATTERS ON
BEING A CHRISTIAN TODAY

[Editor's Note: The answers to questions printed here were given by Lewis at a 'One Man Brains Trust' held on April 18, 1944, at the Head Office of Electric and Musical Industries Ltd., Hayes, Middlesex. Shorthand notes were made and a typescript was sent to Lewis. He revised it a little, and it was printed in 1944. Mr. H. W. Bowen was the question-master.]

LEWIS: I have been asked to open with a few words on Christianity and modern industry. Now mod-

---

God in the Dock, from the chapter titled
"Answers to Questions on Christianity."

ern industry is a subject of which I know nothing at all. But for that very reason it may illustrate what Christianity, in my opinion, does and does not do. Christianity *does not* replace the technical. When it tells you to feed the hungry it doesn't give you lessons in cookery. If you want to learn *that*, you must go to a cook rather than a Christian. If you are not a professional economist and have no experience of industry, simply being a Christian won't give you the answer to industrial problems. My own idea is that modern industry is a radically hopeless system. You can improve wages, hours, conditions, etc., but all that doesn't cure the deepest trouble, i.e., that numbers of people are kept all their lives doing dull repetition work which gives no full play to their faculties. How that is to be overcome, I do not know. If a single country abandoned the system it would merely fall a prey to the other countries which hadn't abandoned it. I don't know the solution: that is not the kind of thing Christianity teaches a person like me. Let's now carry on with the questions.

QUESTION 1. Christians are taught to love their neighbours. How, therefore, can they justify their attitude of supporting the war?

LEWIS: You are told to love your neighbour as yourself. How do you love yourself? When I look into my own mind, I find that I do not love myself by thinking myself a dear old chap or having affectionate feelings. I do not think that I love myself because I am particularly good, but just because I am myself and quite apart from my character. I might detest something which I have done. Nevertheless, I do not cease to love myself. In other words, that definite distinction that Christians make between hating sin and loving the sinner is one that you have been making in your own case since you were born. You dislike what you have done, but you don't cease to love yourself. You may even think that you ought to be hanged. You may even think that you ought to go to the police and own up and be hanged. Love is not affectionate feeling, but a steady wish for the loved person's ultimate good as far as it can be obtained. It seems to me, therefore, that when the worst comes to the worst, if you cannot restrain a man by any method except by trying to kill him, then a Christian must do that. That is my answer. But I may be wrong. It is very difficult to answer, of course.

QUESTION 2. Supposing a factory worker asked you: 'How can I find God?' How would you reply?

LEWIS: I don't see how the problem would be different for a factory worker than for anyone else. The primary thing about any man is that he is a human being, sharing all the ordinary human temptations and assets. What is the special problem about the factory worker? But perhaps it is worth saying this:

Christianity really does two things about conditions here and now in this world:

(1) It tries to make them as good as possible, i.e., to reform them; but also

(2) It fortifies you against them insofar as they remain bad.

If what was in the questioner's mind was this problem of repetition work, then the factory worker's difficulty is the same as any other man confronted with any sorrow or difficulty. People will find God if they consciously seek from Him the right attitude toward all unpleasant things . . . if that is the point of the question?

QUESTION 3. Will you please say how you would define a practicing Christian? Are there any other varieties?

LEWIS: Certainly there are a great many other varieties. It depends, of course, on what you mean by 'practising Christian'. If you mean one who has practised Christianity in every respect at every moment of his life, then there is only one on record—Christ Himself. In that sense there are no practising Christians, but only Christians who, in varying degrees, try to practise it and fail in varying degrees and then start again. A perfect practice of Christianity would, of course, consist in a perfect imitation of the life of Christ—I mean, insofar as it was applicable in one's own particular circumstances. Not in an idiotic sense—it doesn't mean that every Christian should grow a beard, or be a bachelor, or become a traveling preacher. It means that every single act and feeling, every experience, whether pleasant or unpleasant, must be referred to God. It means looking at everything as something that comes from Him, and always looking to Him and asking His will first, and saying: 'How would He wish me to deal with this?'

A kind of picture or pattern (in a very remote way) of the relation between the perfect Christian and his God, would be the relation of the good dog to its master. This is only a very imperfect picture, though, because the dog hasn't reason like its master: whereas we do share in God's reason, even if in an imperfect and interrupted way ('interrupted' because we don't think rationally for very long at a time—it's too tiring—and we haven't information to understand things fully, and our intelligence itself has certain limitations). In that way we are more like God than the dog is like us, though, of course, there are other ways in which the dog is more like us than we are like God. It is only an illustration.

QUESTION 4. What justification on ethical grounds and on the grounds of social expediency exists for the church's attitude toward venereal disease and prophylaxis and publicity in connection with it?

LEWIS: I need further advice on that question, and then perhaps I can answer it. Can the questioner say which church he has in mind?

VOICE: The church concerned is the Church of England, and its attitude, though not written, is implicit in that it has more or less banned all publicity in connection with prophylactic methods of combating venereal disease. The view of some is that moral punishment should not be avoided.

LEWIS: I haven't myself met any clergymen of the Church of England who held that view: and I don't hold it myself. There are obvious objections to it. After all, it isn't only venereal disease that can be regarded as a punishment for bad conduct. Indigestion in old age may be the result of overeating in earlier life: but no one objects to advertisements for Beecham's Pills. I, at any rate, strongly dissent from the view you've mentioned.

QUESTION 5. Many people feel resentful or unhappy because they think they are the target of unjust fate. These feelings are stimulated by bereavement, illness, deranged domestic or working conditions, or the observation of suffering in others. What is the Christian view of this problem?

LEWIS: The Christian view is that men were created to be in a certain relationship to God (if we are in that relation to Him, the right relation to one another will follow inevitably). Christ said it was difficult for 'the rich' to enter the Kingdom of Heaven,[1] referring, no doubt, to 'riches' in the ordinary sense. But I think it really covers riches in every sense—good fortune, health, popularity, and all the things one wants to have. All these things tend—just as money tends—to make you feel independent of God, because if you have them you are happy already and contented in this life. You don't want to turn away to anything more, and so you try to rest in a shadowy happiness as if it could last forever. But God wants to give you a real and eternal happiness. Consequently He may have to take all these 'riches' away from you: if He doesn't, you will go on relying on them. It sounds cruel, doesn't it? But I am beginning to find out that what people call the cruel doctrines are really the kindest ones in the long run. I used to think it was a 'cruel' doctrine to say that troubles and sorrows were 'punishments'. But I find in practice that when you are in trouble, the moment you regard it as a 'punishment', it becomes easier to bear. If you think of this world as a place intended simply for our happiness, you find it quite intolerable: think of it as a place of training and correction and it's not so bad.

Imagine a set of people all living in the same building. Half of them think it is a hotel, the other half think it is a prison. Those who think it a hotel might regard it as quite intolerable, and those who thought it was a prison might decide that it was really surprisingly comfortable. So that what seems the ugly doctrine is one that comforts and strengthens you in the end. The people who try to hold an optimistic view of this world would become pessimists: the people who hold a pretty stern view of it become optimistic.

QUESTION 6. Materialists and some astronomers suggest that the solar planetary system and life as we know it was brought about by an accidental stellar collision. What is the Christian view of this theory?

LEWIS: If the solar system was brought about by an accidental collision, then the appearance of organic life on this planet was also an accident, and the whole evolution of man was an accident too. If so, then all our present thoughts are mere accidents—the accidental by-product of the movement of atoms. And this holds for the thoughts of the materialists and astronomers as well as for anyone else's. But if *their* thoughts—i.e., of materialism and astronomy—are merely accidental by-products, why should we believe them to be true? I see no reason for believing that one accident should be able to give me a correct account of all the other accidents. It's like expecting that the accidental shape taken by the splash when you upset a milk jug should give you a correct account of how the jug was made and why it was upset.

QUESTION 7. Is it true that Christianity (especially the Protestant forms) tends to produce a gloomy, joyless condition of society which is like a pain in the neck to most people?

LEWIS: As to the distinction between Protestant and other forms of Christianity, it is very difficult to answer. I find by reading about the sixteenth century, that people like Sir Thomas More, for whom I have a great respect, always regarded Martin Luther's doctrines not as gloomy thinking, but as wishful thinking. I doubt whether we can make a distinction between Protestant and other forms in this respect. Whether Protestantism is gloomy and whether Christianity at all produces gloominess, I find it very difficult to answer, as I have never lived in a completely non-Christian society nor a completely Christian one, and I wasn't there in the sixteenth century, and only have my knowledge from reading books. I think there is about the same amount of fun and gloom in all periods. The poems, novels, letters, etc., of every period all seem to show that. But again, I don't really know the answer, of course. I wasn't there.

QUESTION 8. Is it true that Christians must be prepared to live a life of personal discomfort and self-sacrifice in order to qualify for 'Pie in the Sky'?

LEWIS: All people, whether Christian or not, must be prepared to live a life of discomfort. It is impossible to accept Christianity for the sake of finding comfort: but the Christian tries to lay himself open to the will of God, to do what God wants him to do. You don't know in advance whether God is going to set you to do something difficult or painful, or something that you will quite like; and some people of heroic mould are disappointed when the job doled out to them turns out to be something quite nice. But you must be prepared for the unpleasant things and the discomforts. I don't mean fasting, and things like that. They are a different matter. When you are training soldiers in manoeuvres, you practise in blank ammunition because you would like them to have practice before meeting the real enemy. So we must practice in abstaining from pleasures which are not in themselves wicked. If you don't abstain from pleasure, you won't be good when the time comes along. It is purely a matter of practice.

VOICE: Are not practises like fasting and self-denial borrowed from earlier or more primitive religions?

LEWIS: I can't say for certain which bits came into Christianity from earlier religions. An enormous amount did. I should find it hard to believe Christianity if that were not so. I couldn't believe that nine hundred and ninety-nine religions were completely false and the remaining one true. In reality, Christianity is primarily the fulfillment of the Jewish religion, but also the fulfillment of what was vaguely hinted in all the religions at their best. What was vaguely seen in them all comes into focus in Christianity—just as God Himself comes into focus by becoming a man. I take it that the speaker's remarks on earlier religions are based on evidence about modern savages. I don't think it is good evidence. Modern savages usually represent some decay in culture—you find them doing things which look as if they had a fairly civilized basis once, which they have forgotten. To assume that primitive man was exactly like the modern savage is unsound.

VOICE: Could you say any more on how one discovers whether a task is laid on one by God, or whether it comes in some other way? If we cannot distinguish between the pleasant and the unpleasant things, it is a complicated matter.

LEWIS: We are guided by the ordinary rules of moral behaviour, which I think are more or less common to the human race and quite reasonable and demanded by the circumstances. I don't mean anything like sitting down and waiting for a supernatural vision.

VOICE: We don't qualify for heaven by practise, but salvation is obtained at the Cross. We do nothing to obtain it, but follow Christ. We may have pain or tribulation, but nothing we do qualifies us for heaven, but Christ.

LEWIS: The controversy about faith and works is one that has gone on for a very long time, and it is a highly technical matter. I personally rely on the paradoxical text: 'Work out your own salvation . . . for it is God that worketh in you.'[2] It looks as if in one sense we do nothing, and in another case we do a damned lot. 'Work out your own salvation with fear and trembling',[3] but you must have it in you before you can work it out. But I have no wish to go further into it, as it would interest no one but the Christians present, would it?

QUESTION 9. Would the application of Christian standards bring to an end or greatly reduce scientific and material progress? In other words, is it wrong for a Christian to be ambitious and strive for personal success?

LEWIS: It is easiest to think of a simplified example. How would the application of Christianity affect anyone on a desert island? Would he be less likely to build a comfortable hut? The answer is 'No'. There might come a particular moment, of course, when Christianity would tell him to bother less about the hut, i.e., if he were in danger of coming to think that the hut was the most important thing in the universe.

But there is no evidence that Christianity would prevent him from building it.

Ambition! We must be careful what we mean by it. If it means the desire to get ahead of other people—which is what I think it does mean—then it is bad. If it means simply wanting to do a thing well, then it is good. It isn't wrong for an actor to want to act his part as well as it can possibly be acted, but the wish to have his name in bigger type than the other actors is a bad one.

VOICE: It's all right to be a general, but if it is one's ambition to be a general, then you shouldn't become one.

LEWIS: The mere event of becoming a general isn't either right or wrong in itself. What matters morally is your attitude toward it. The man may be thinking about winning a war; he may be wanting to be a general because he honestly thinks he has a good plan and is glad of a chance to carry it out. That's all right. But if he is thinking: 'What can I get out of the job?' or 'How can I get on the front page of the *Illustrated*

News?' then it is all wrong. And what we call 'ambition' usually means the wish to be more conspicuous or more successful than someone else. It is this competitive element in it that is bad. It is perfectly reasonable to want to dance well or to look nice. But when the dominant wish is to dance better or look nicer than the others—when you begin to feel that if the others danced as well as you or looked as nice as you, that would take all the fun out of it—then you are going wrong.

VOICE: I am wondering how far we can ascribe to the work of the Devil those very legitimate desires that we indulge in. Some people have a very sensitive conception of the presence of the Devil. Others haven't. Is the Devil as real as we think he is? That doesn't trouble some people, since they have no desire to be good, but others are continually harassed by the Old Man himself.

LEWIS: No reference to the Devil or devils is included in any Christian Creeds, and it is quite possible to be a Christian without believing in them. I do believe such beings exist, but that is my own affair. Supposing there to be such beings, the degree to which humans were conscious of their presence would presumably vary very much. I mean, the more a man was in the Devil's power, the less he would be aware of it, on the principle that a man is still fairly sober as long as he knows he's drunk. It is the people who are fully awake and trying hard to be good who would be most aware of the Devil. It is when you start arming against Hitler that you first realise your country is full of Nazi agents. Of course, they don't want you to believe in the Devil. If devils exist, their first aim is to give you an anesthetic—to put you off your guard. Only if that fails, do you become aware of them.

VOICE: Does Christianity retard scientific advancement? Or does it approve of those who help spiritually others who are on the road to perdition, by scientifically removing the environmental causes of the trouble?

LEWIS: Yes. In the abstract it is certainly so. At a particular moment, if most human beings are concentrating only on material improvements in the environment, it may be the duty of Christians to point out (and pretty loudly) that this isn't the only thing that matters. But as a general rule it is in favour of all knowledge and all that will help the human race in any way.

QUESTION 10. The Bible was written thousands of years ago for people in a lower state of mental development than today. Many portions seem preposterous in the light of modern knowledge. In view of this, should not the Bible be rewritten with the object of discarding the fabulous and reinterpreting the remainder?

LEWIS: First of all as to the people in a lower state of mental development. I am not so sure what lurks behind that. If it means that people ten thousand years ago didn't know a good many things that we know now, of course, I agree. But if it means that there has been any advance in *intelligence* in that time, I believe there is no evidence for any such thing. The Bible can be divided into two parts—the Old and the New Testaments. The Old Testament contains fabulous elements. The New Testament consists mostly of teaching, not of narrative at all: but where it *is* narrative, it is, in my opinion, historical. As to the fabulous element in the Old Testament, I very much doubt if you would be wise to chuck it out. What you get is something *coming gradually into focus*. First you get, scattered through the heathen religions all over the world—but still quite vague and mythical—the idea of a god who is killed and broken and then comes to life again. No one knows where he is supposed to have lived and died; he's not historical. Then you get the Old Testament. Religious ideas get a bit more focused. Everything is now connected with a particular nation. And it comes still more into focus as it goes on. Jonah and the Whale,[4] Noah and his Ark,[5] are fabulous; but the court history of King David[6] is probably as reliable as the court history of Louis XIV. Then, in the New Testament the *thing really happens*.

The dying God really appears—as an historical person, living in a definite place and time. If we *could* sort out all the fabulous elements in the earlier stages and separate them from the historical ones, I think we might lose an essential part of the whole process. That is my own idea.

QUESTION 11. Which of the religions of the world gives to its followers the greatest happiness?

LEWIS: Which of the religions of the world gives to its followers the greatest happiness? While it lasts, the religion of worshiping oneself is the best.

I have an elderly acquaintance of about eighty, who has lived a life of unbroken selfishness and self-admiration from the earliest years, and is, more or less, I regret to say, one of the happiest men I know. From the moral point of view it is very difficult! I am not approaching the question from that angle. As you perhaps know, I haven't always been a Christian. I didn't go to religion to make me happy. I always knew a bottle of port would do that. If you want a religion to make you feel really comfortable, I certainly don't recommend Christianity. I am certain there must be a patent American article on the market which will suit you far better, but I can't give any advice on it.

QUESTION 12. Are there any unmistakable outward signs in a person surrendered to God? Would he be cantankerous? Would he smoke?

LEWIS: I think of the advertisements for 'White Smiles' toothpaste, saying that it is the best on the market. If they are true, it would follow that:

(1) Anyone who starts using it will have better teeth;

(2) Anyone using it has better teeth than he would have if he weren't using it.

But you can't test it in the case of one who has naturally bad teeth and uses it, and compare him with a healthy primitive who has never used toothpaste at all.

Take the case of a sour old maid, who is a Christian, but cantankerous. On the other hand, take some pleasant and popular fellow, but who has never been to church. Who knows how much more cantankerous the old maid might be if she were *not* a Christian, and how much more likable the nice fellow might be if he *were* a Christian? You can't judge Christianity simply by comparing the *product* in those two people; you would need to know what kind of raw material Christ was working on in both cases.

As an illustration, let us take a case of industrialism. Let us take two factories:

Factory A with poor and inadequate plant, and

Factory B with first-class modern plant.

You can't judge by the outside. You must consider the plant and methods by which they are run, and considering the plant at Factory A, it may be a wonder it does anything at all; and considering the new machinery at Factory B, it may be a wonder it doesn't do better.

QUESTION 13. What is your opinion about raffles within the plant—no matter how good the cause—which, not infrequently, is given less prominence than the alluring list of prizes?

LEWIS: Gambling ought never to be an important part of a man's life. If it is a way in which large sums of money are transferred from person to person without doing any good (e.g., producing employment, goodwill, etc.) then it is a bad thing. If it is carried out on a small scale, I am not sure that it is bad. I don't know much about it, because it is about the only vice to which I have no temptation at all, and I think it is a risk to talk about things which are not in my own makeup, because I don't understand them. If anyone comes to me asking to play bridge for money, I just say: 'How much do you hope to win? Take it and go away.'

QUESTION 14. Many people are quite unable to understand the theological differences which have caused divisions in the Christian Church. Do you consider that these differences are fundamental, and is the time now ripe for reunion?

LEWIS: The time is always ripe for reunion. Divisions between Christians are a sin and a scandal, and Christians ought at all times to be making contributions toward reunion, if it is only by their prayers. I am only a layman and a recent Christian, and I do not know much about these things, but in all the things which I have written and thought I have always stuck to traditional, dogmatic positions. The result is that letters of agreement reach me from what are ordinarily regarded as the most different kinds of Christians; for instance, I get letters from Jesuits, monks, nuns, and also from Quakers and Welsh Dissenters, and so on. So it seems to me that the 'extremist' elements in every church are nearest one another and the liberal and 'broad-minded' people in each body could never be united at all. The world of dogmatic Christianity is a place in which thousands of people of quite different types keep on saying the same thing, and the world of 'broad-mindedness' and watered-down 'religion' is a world where a small number of people (all of the same type) say totally different things and change their minds every few minutes. We shall never get reunion from them.

QUESTION 15. In the past the church used various kinds of compulsion in attempts to force a particular brand of Christianity on the community. Given sufficient power, is there not a danger of this sort of thing happening again?

LEWIS: Yes, I hear nasty rumours coming from Spain. Persecution is a temptation to which all men are exposed. I had a postcard signed 'M. D.' saying that anyone who expressed and published his belief in the Virgin Birth should be stripped and flogged. That shows you how easily persecution of Christians by the non-Christians might come back. Of course, they wouldn't call it persecution: they'd call it 'compulsory reeducation of the ideologically unfit', or something like that. But, of course, I have to admit that Christians themselves have been persecutors in the past. It was worse of them, because *they* ought to have known better: they weren't worse in any other way. I detest every kind of religious compulsion: only the other day I was writing an angry letter to *The Spectator* about church parades in the Home Guard!

QUESTION 16. Is attendance at a place of worship or membership with a Christian community necessary to a Christian way of life?

LEWIS: That's a question which I cannot answer. My own experience is that when I first became a Christian, about fourteen years ago, I thought that I could do it on my own, by retiring to my rooms and reading theology, and I wouldn't go to the churches and Gospel halls; and then later I found that it was the only way of flying your flag; and, of course, I found that this meant being a target. It is extraordinary how inconvenient to your family it becomes for you to get up early to go to church. It doesn't matter so much if you get up early for anything else, but if you get up early to go to church it's very selfish of you and you upset the house. If there is anything in the teaching of the New Testament which is in the nature of a command, it is that you are obliged to take the Sacrament,[7] and you can't do it without going to church. I disliked very much their hymns, which I considered to be fifth-rate poems set to sixth-rate music. But as I went on I saw the great merit of it. I came up against different people of quite different outlooks and different education, and then gradually my conceit just began peeling off. I realised that the hymns (which were just sixth-rate music) were, nevertheless, being sung with devotion and benefit by an old saint in elastic-side boots in the opposite pew, and then you realise that you aren't fit to clean those boots. It gets you out of your solitary conceit. It is not for me to lay down laws, as I am only a layman, and I don't know much.

QUESTION 17. If it is true that one has only to want God enough in order to find Him, how can I make myself want Him enough to enable myself to find Him?

LEWIS: If you don't want God, why are you so anxious to want to want Him? I think that in reality the want is a real one, and I should say that this person has in fact found God, although it may not be fully recognized yet. We are not always aware of things at the time they happen. At any rate, what is more important is that God has found this person, and that is the main thing.

[1] Matthew 19:23; Mark 10:23; Luke 18:24.

[2] Philippians 2:12.

[3] *Ibid*.

[4] The Book of Jonah.

[5] Genesis, chapters 6–8.

[6] II Samuel, ch. 2—I Kings, ch. 2.

[7] John 6:53–54: 'Except ye eat the flesh of the Son of man, and drink his blood, ye have no life in you. Whoso eateth my flesh, and drinketh my blood, hath eternal life; and I will raise him up at the last day'.

SOURCE WORKS

Christian Reflections, Eerdmans; ebook, HarperOne.
- "On Doubts and the Gift of Faith" is from the chapter titled "Religion: Reality or Substitute?"

God in the Dock: Essays on Theology and Ethics, Eerdmans; ebook, HarperOne.
- "On the Dangers of Pointing Out Faults in Others" is from the chapter titled "'The Trouble with "X". . .'."
- "On Denying Oneself While Loving Oneself" is from the chapter titled "Two Ways with the Self."
- "On the Appeal and Challenges of Home Life" is from the chapter titled "The Sermon and the Lunch."
- "On Not Feeling Threatened When Christianity Remains Unchanged While Science and Knowledge Progresses" is from the chapter titled "Dogma and the Universe."
- "On Practical Matters on Being a Christian Today" is from the chapter titled "Answers to Questions on Christianity."

Mere Christianity, HarperOne.
- "On Working Out Your Salvation" is from the chapter titled "Faith."
- "On How We Spread the Christ-Life Within" is from the chapter titled "The Practical Conclusion."
- "On the Importance of Practicing Charity" is from the chapter titled "Charity."

Present Concerns: Journalistic Essays, HarperOne.
- "On What It Means to Say, 'To Live Is Christ'" is from the chapter titled "Three Kinds of Men."

The Weight of Glory and Other Addresses, HarperOne.
- "On Being Concerned About More Than the Salvation of Souls" is from the chapter titled "Learning in War-Time."
- "On Forgiveness as a Necessary Practice" is from the chapter titled "On Forgiveness."
- "On the Christian Art of Attaining Glory" is from the chapter titled "The Weight of Glory."
- "On What It Means to Be Part of the Body of Christ" is from the chapter titled "Membership."

The World's Last Night and Other Essays, HarperOne.
- "On Living Today While Expecting the Second Coming Tomorrow" is from the chapter titled "The World's Last Night."

DISCOVER C. S. LEWIS

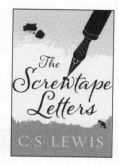